The Single Girl's Guide to

MARRYING A MAN,

HIS KIDS,

AND

HIS EX-WIFE

Sally Bjornsen

The Single Girl's Guide to

MARRYING A MAN,

HIS KIDS,

AND

HIS EX-WIFE

Becoming a Stepmother with
Humor and Grace

 NEW AMERICAN LIBRARY

New American Library
Published by New American Library, a division of
Penguin Group (USA) Inc., 375 Hudson Street,
New York, New York 10014, USA
Penguin Group (Canada), 10 Alcorn Avenue, Toronto,
Ontario M4V 3B2, Canada (a division of Pearson Penguin Canada Inc.)
Penguin Books Ltd., 80 Strand, London WC2R 0RL, England
Penguin Ireland, 25 St. Stephen's Green, Dublin 2,
Ireland (a division of Penguin Books Ltd.)
Penguin Group (Australia), 250 Camberwell Road, Camberwell, Victoria 3124,
Australia (a division of Pearson Australia Group Pty. Ltd.)
Penguin Books India Pvt. Ltd., 11 Community Centre, Panchsheel Park,
New Delhi – 110 017, India
Penguin Group (NZ), cnr Airborne and Rosedale Roads, Albany,
Auckland 1310, New Zealand (a division of Pearson New Zealand Ltd.)
Penguin Books (South Africa) (Pty.) Ltd., 24 Sturdee Avenue,
Rosebank, Johannesburg 2196, South Africa

Penguin Books Ltd., Registered Offices: 80 Strand, London WC2R 0RL, England

First published by New American Library, a division of Penguin Group (USA) Inc.

First Printing, April 2005
10 9 8 7 6 5 4 3 2 1

Copyright © Sally Bjornsen, 2005
All rights reserved

NEW AMERICAN LIBRARY and logo are trademarks of Penguin Group (USA) Inc.

LIBRARY OF CONGRESS CATALOGING-IN-PUBLICATION DATA:
Bjornsen, Sally.
The single girl's guide to marrying a man, his kids and his ex-wife :
becoming a stepmother with humor and grace / Sally Bjornsen.
p. cm.
ISBN 0-451-21419-6 (trade pbk.)
1. Stepmothers.   I. Title.
HQ759.92.B54 2005
306.874'7—dc22

2004021836

Set in Mrs. Eaves Roman
Designed by Jennifer Ann Daddio

Printed in the United States of America

TO MY BOYS

Acknowledgments

The Single Girl's Guide to Marrying a Man, His Kids, and His Ex-Wife would not have been possible without the many successful sassy stepmothers who believed in this book and who were willing to give me the straight scoop about being a stepmother. You are all inspirations to me.

Furthermore, this book would never have made it past the idea phase had it not been for the encouragement of my brilliant and witty friends Portia Langworthy and Sean O'Conner, who were always there to tell me what was and wasn't funny. And for Kerrie Foss, Whitney Whiton, and Waverly Fitzgerald, who kept me honest, inspired, and politically correct.

I give great thanks to my agent and cheerleader, Laurie Abekmeier, who not only embraced the idea of *The Single Girl's Guide to Marrying a Man, His Kids, and His Ex-Wife*, but also was willing to tutor me on the intricate details of the publishing world. And to my editor Christine Zika, who believed in the book so much she wanted to publish it.

Acknowledgments

To Susan, for whom I have great respect and appreciation, thank you for giving me the opportunity to love your
sons.

And to my boys, all three of them: It is your laughter,
spontaneity and support that makes my world go 'round.

Lastly, thanks to my husband, who saw something in me
early on that made him think I'd be a good stepmother.
Thank you for your undying confidence, patience, and
sense of humor.

Contents

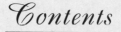

The Single Girl's Guide to

MARRYING A MAN,

HIS KIDS,

AND

HIS EX-WIFE

INTRODUCTION:

The Ride of Your Life

*C*ongratulations. If you're reading this book, you are likely a new or soon-to-be new step-mother and wife. Hold on—because this is going to be the wildest ride of your life. And like most wild rides it will scare the hell out of you and make you laugh your tail off—all at the same time.

When I got married a few years ago, the media had just released a rash of reports on the dismal outlook for any woman over thirty hoping to get married. According to experts, I was in my marital sunset years and damn lucky to have landed a living, breathing straight man who wasn't drooling or in need of a sugar mama. I could hardly believe my good fortune. My husband-to-be was handsome and tall, which served my need to feel thin and small. He was nuts about me and laughed at most of my jokes. But there was one minor detail: My knight had a small family complete with two boys and an ex-wife nearby. Love-struck and relieved that there was still at least one good guy

left, I willingly overlooked what seemed like mere minu-
tiae at the time and pursued the relationship with gusto!

Within four months of our meeting, Mark, my soon-
to-be fiancé, and his little township moved into my one-
bedroom nine-hundred-square-foot condo. It was bliss.
When his boys weren't with us, we basked in the glow of
new love. When they were with us (one-third of the time),
Mark and I slept like sardines on a borrowed futon in the
living room while the boys slept like snoring rocks in the
bedroom. It was an ongoing slumber party. Within a year
we were all happily engaged. But a year later and many
months into our marriage, the slumber party came to a
screeching halt. I was ready to scream "uncle," as well as
some other choice expletives.

Distraught that I wasn't enamored with my role as a
stepmother, I sought some practical counsel from friends
and family on the dos and don'ts of keeping the romance
while helping to raise someone else's kids. Much to my
chagrin I found that no one in my circle of confidants had
any helpful advice because they hadn't been there. I was
further stunned to find so few books written on the topic.

After several trips to the bookstore and the library, I
found a few tomes that tackled the stepmother subject
buried among the many self-help books written on biological parenting, childbirth, and divorce. With the exception of *The Complete Idiot's Guide to Stepparenting* (which
targeted idiot stepmothers), most books were written for
discouraged stepmothers on the brink of disaster or, at
the very least, divorce. It was depressing!

Disappointed by the lack of written guidance, I sought
out a local stepmother support group. Six of us sat in a

circle as the facilitator encouraged us to spill our stories of crisis and frustration. I left feeling turned off and glad I hadn't attended the group before I agreed to get married. Instead of tales of woe, I wanted to hear about the seven, twelve, or sixteen steps for stepmother success. What I needed was a savvy stepmother role model. A Carol Brady or Maria Von Trapp with a sense of humor—a fresh-faced stepmother who actually liked being one.

With few options and no role model, I tried to construct the steps to success on my own, making them up and trying them out as I stumbled along. Now, years later, I still occasionally slip and fall, but most of the time I'm amazed at how much enjoyment and satisfaction I get from my ready-made family.

The Single Girl's Guide to Marrying a Man, His Kids, and His Ex-Wife is written for you, the budding stepmother and wife. I hope it can give you the support, camaraderie, and inspiration that I longed for in those first few years of marriage and stepmotherhood. While I can't personally meet you for coffee to brag about stepkids or to advise you about how to behave at Little League games or piano recitals, I can offer you some honest and straightforward firsthand guidance from a seasoned pro and the dozens of sassy stepmother friends I interviewed. So please sit back, pour yourself a glass of wine, and enjoy the ride.

CHAPTER ONE

Stepmotherhood 101

*W*hat to Expect When You're Expecting is the bible for soon-to-be biological moms (aka bio-moms). Over the years I have purchased at least four copies of this highly acclaimed book of advice for inexperienced friends and relatives who have found themselves in the mothering way. When I gleefully announced that I was in the "stepmothering way," there was no de facto stepmothering guide for me. Instead of a manual of advice on how to raise someone else's children, my friends gave me a bottle of wine and a diary and toasted me with something akin to "Glad it's you and not me."

Unlike our bio-mom counterparts, stepmothers have no gestation period to get used to the idea of becoming a parent. There is no nine-month primer filled with congratulations and grandmotherly advice, no strangers patting your tummy or time-tested counsel from Dr. Spock. There are no stepmother showers, no books with chatty stepmother advice (except this one), and no tuna noodle casseroles on the doorstep. Instead we go into the role blindly, without any tutelage from friends, books, or doctors.

A Sense of Humor Is a Stepmother's Best Friend

Now after years of making my share of stepmothering faux pas, I have become, within my social circle, the consummate expert on the topic. My qualifications are few: I am relatively sane, still crazy about my husband, and usually amused and enchanted (and occasionally enraged) by my sweet and sometimes evil stepsons. It is this list of qualifications that prompts the question from women of all ages: "How do you do it?" I often wonder if this is a rhetorical question or if the questioner is truly looking for a magical answer. Regardless, I have worked up my signature response to the inquiry. First I offer a sly smile and then I say, with the proud confidence of a seasoned professional, "With a sense of humor, my dear."

People tend to ask me this question under their breath, usually at a Little League game or school function when the ex-wife is a few bodies down on the bleachers—a mere spitting distance away. The good news is I no longer want to spit on her or let the air out of her tires when I see her. Actually, violence is not my style. I am drawn, instead, to a more subtle approach—catty mischievousness and silent brooding. But as the years progress I have fewer impulses to display malicious manners and spiteful sarcasm. I have finally matured and learned to accept my new family, the whole lot, including my stepchildren, the ex-wife, her new husband, his ex-wife, and his kids. In fact I've designed a handy little flowchart to show confused acquaintances who innocently ask, "Now, whose boys are these?"

As I pat myself on the back for my new adult point of view, I must admit that I didn't always have this perspective. In fact, I can say looking back that I was terribly immature during our first year of marriage. Too bad for me—a sense of humor and a mature attitude would have saved me some embarrassing moments and sleepless nights. Not to mention given me more free time to chase my husband around the bedroom naked like a newlywed should.

The only excuse I have for my wacky behavior that first year is that we had a schizophrenic life. We were wild honeymooners every other weekend and overworked parents on those in between. I was the light of my husband's life when we didn't have the kids, and the forgotten toy at the bottom of the toy box when they showed up. I had no one to consult on my double life and virtually no firsthand experience as a wife or mother. It is no wonder I lost my sense of humor every other weekend!

But I made it through that first year of stepmother boot camp without getting discharged or going AWOL. I have developed some thick skin along the way, but I am proud to say that the experience has made me a much more interesting and well-rounded person. For example, when I first met Mark and his boys, I didn't know the difference between a split-fingered fastball and a sidearm slider. Now, thanks to Guy, my oldest stepson, I can give a play-by-play recap of a major-league baseball game complete with pitching analysis. In turn I have enlightened him on the game within the game, including salacious scoop on players' personal lives and the impact of astrological sun signs on the game. "Guy, what you must know is that a player's astrological sign is as worthy a statistic as his RBI. The probability of a player's striking out is largely based on his rising sign." My lectures are always met with rolling eyes and a standard heartwarming response, "Sally, you're so weird."

Baseball knowledge is not all I have learned while comothering my husband's brood. I am pleased to say that it has taught me to take multitasking to a whole new level. It is not uncommon for me to navigate my station wagon full of preteen boys from one Little League playing field to another while composing original rap tunes and applying lipstick. I have learned to build my own version of LEGOLAND in our living room, recite lines from *Wallace and Gromit*, and comfort a crying boy. But most astonishing is the fact that I can have an adult conversation at a piano recital with the woman who slept with my hunky husband for twelve years and not clench my jaw, roll my eyes, or plot her demise.

Sassy Stepmother Straight Scoop

So how do you do it? you ask. April, a wise stepmother friend of mine from Alabama, says it best (imagine a Southern drawl). "My motto to all future stepmothers is, You have to laugh to keep from crying!" Many of the happy stepmothers I have gabbed with over the years tell me the same thing: You have to have a sense of humor, a strong sense of self, and a good inventory of fine wine to make it as a not-so-evil stepmother. Even the women I know who have painlessly slipped into the role have had their feelings hurt along the way. It goes with the territory. If it is any consolation, keep in mind that most of the problems you encounter with your stepkids and your husband's ex-wife are likely about them and not about you.

His Kids Come First—Learning to Love Second Place

My stepmother friend Laura is famous for recounting some advice she was given by an old relative right before she married her husband and his two kids. It went something like this:"Dawling, prepare yourself. Because no matter what, when you marry a man with children, his kids will always come first." My friend recoiled at the old broad's callous advice. At the time, the bride-to-be was twenty-thousand dollars into the wedding and there was no turning back. Instead of canceling the caterer, she picked up the phone, called her mother, and had the old biddy removed from the guest list.

While Laura was able to erase the advice-giving grandma from her wedding day, she was not able to erase the words of wisdom from her head. Eventually, after a few years of marriage and stepmotherhood, she came to understand where the stepmother scrooge was coming from. To this day, she is unashamed of imparting similar advice to the uninitiated stepmommy-to-be. Unfortunately, my friend's hard-earned advice was lost on me. "My situation is different," I told myself. It was a lesson I had to learn firsthand.

One day in my new family's first year together, we were out Christmas shopping downtown. My older stepson, Guy, seven years old at the time and the consummate negotiator, was trying to put together a deal with his dad— something about LEGOs for labor. I commented on his pitch, "Guy, your negotiating technique is not helping you close the deal. Cut out the whining and talk like a big boy." Annoyed by my attempt to add some humorous instruction, Guy stuck out his foot and tripped me. I fell face-first onto the pavement. Guy was shocked when he turned to see me sprawled on the sidewalk with my handbag and its contents lying in the gutter. "What are you, possessed? You snotty brat!" I hissed through tears and a clenched jaw. My words shamed him, and he began to cry. Passing shoppers with overstuffed shopping bags stared as I struggled on hands and knees to gather my rolling lipsticks, ballpoint pens, and runaway tampons. Mark stood frozen as he took in the sight: me, on all fours, cursing like a drunk and picking rocks out of my bloody palms, Guy sobbing. Stymied, I watched as Mark chose to calm Guy with a giant bear hug rather than rescue me from the pavement.

On the drive home I fumed with rage. I was so incensed that, for the first time in my life, I could not speak—probably a blessing given the fact that there were children in the car. Instead, I silently entertained the idea of giving my husband a stiff karate chop to his bad knee and hanging my evil stepson by his toenails.

Later that night, I miraculously recovered from my mute state and rediscovered vocal cords that rivaled those of Maria Callas. On hands and knees I reenacted for Mark the tripping disaster over and over to make my point. "How could you leave me stranded face-first on the ground in front of Nordstrom?" I wailed. "I thought you loved me!" I shouted. "He tripped me!" I whined again, exaggerating trip-and-fall motions like a professional mime.

No matter how much drama and rationale I used, Mark kept coming back to his original defense. "I am so sorry I didn't go to you first, but you called my son a possessed brat, Sally. He's only seven years old." Mark didn't seem to care that I would not have called his son a possessed brat if he hadn't tripped me in the first place. Exhausted by my failed performance, I went to bed feeling like I was the one who had done something terribly wrong.

The next day Mark had a man-to-man discussion with Guy about the inappropriateness of tripping one's stepmother. His calm and rational manner must have worked because I haven't been tripped by anyone except myself since.

Sassy Stepmother Straight Scoop

Our Tripgate disaster of 1999 taught me the kids-come-first lesson. Here's the deal: Good men, the kind you want to share the rest of your life with, feel guilty about putting their children through the pain of divorce. They will try for the remainder of their lives to make it up to their children. As a result, a divorced man who is a conscientious father will often put his kids before you. It doesn't mean he loves you any less than he does his children. The sooner you grasp this lesson, the easier your life will be. It doesn't give your stepchildren the green light to mistreat you, but if it comes to a fight between you and them, your husband is likely to give them the benefit of the doubt.

Expect to Get Mad

While it may be human nature for your husband to defend his little terrorists when they are being monstrous, it doesn't make it any easier for you. In fact, as I know from experience, it hurts—a lot. In times like this, you may be tempted to declare domestic jihad against your family. You may even have shameful fantasies of retribution—for example, imposing indefinite time-outs, running away with the studly personal trainer at the gym, or simply jabbing your husband in the eye with a hot poker. Two words of comfort: *very normal*. But remember one thing: A fitful, evil rage is rarely flattering. Instead, implement the following two-part plan for a peaceful household.

REMAIN CALM AND COUNT
TO NINE THOUSAND

I don't do calm. It's not in my nature. Instead I use my own ready-made technique that has come in very handy in my role as a stepmother. It's called Get Out of Dodge Before You Say Something You'll Regret. Whether that means escaping the confines of the home I share with my husband and his darlings or simply going to the bedroom and shutting the door, I make sure I get away—far away.

Take as long as you need to gather your wits, punch a pillow, curse your head off, or vent to a girlfriend. Whatever it takes. Just don't take out your frustration on the children because, well, they are children. When you are ready to speak rationally and logically, have a conversation with your husband—alone. Together come up with a plan to address the consequences of your stepchild's actions.

FACE YOUR DEMONS!

Once you and your husband have discussed the "incident" and have devised a plan to avoid a repeat performance, you will need to face the perpetrator—alone. In a calm and even tone tell him that his behavior made you feel rotten. Let him know in no uncertain terms that such behavior will not be tolerated. And then, after time has passed and the dust settles, give the kid a heartfelt hug.

When I first got married I ran, like a wounded toddler, to my husband whenever there was a conflict with the kids. I'd demand, "You need to tell them that they can't treat me this way!" What I quickly learned was that Mark became the one to own the authority in our house. Without him by my side, I couldn't fight my own battles. Instead I was reduced to the role of sibling rather than parent. I have learned that it is much more effective to deal with my stepchildren straight on rather than to pass the buck. As a result I have gained more respect from both the children and my man.

Expect to Be Evil Now and Then

"You are the best evil stepmother in the universe!" Music to my ears. My charming stepsons have given new meaning to the title "evil stepmother." Instead of a reference to the wart-nosed character in *Snow White and the Seven Dwarfs*, it has become their personal brand of endearment. I imagine that someday when I pass away, they will shed tears over my grave while blubbering through a heartfelt eulogy that reads, "She was a kind and loving evil stepmother."

An oxymoron? Not really. Evilness goes with the territory of stepmotherhood, much like it does with bio-parenting, except you feel more wicked and vulnerable when you're thinking bad thoughts about someone else's kids. When I was growing up there were times when I was downright hideous to my mother and vice versa, but we both knew that our lifelong relationship could tolerate tornado-like conflicts, and that love would eventually prevail. The relationship between a stepparent and a stepchild is not as absolute.

Furthermore, I have discovered that I have a much lower threshold for bad behavior from my stepsons than my husband or his ex-wife do. I think something happens to parents when they give birth to a baby: I call it the "You're so cute you can do no wrong" bond. When you parent someone else's child, you simply don't have the same bond. A snotty attitude combined with a "You're not the boss of me" comment takes on a whole new meaning when you're the stepmother.

The stepmother role is designed to drive an otherwise kind woman to evildom whether she likes it or not. Allow me to paint the picture for you: You, you rare and deli-cate flower, fall in love with a beautiful and thoughtful man. He has kids. "I can handle it," you tell yourself. You embrace your role with enthusiasm and vigor, laying your heart on the line.

The kids, bless their hearts, like you OK, but they're not always nice to you. In fact, sometimes they're down-right sinful—even when you've read them bedtime stories, scratched their backs, let them stay up way past their bed-time, and generously pitched in for child support.

And the bio-mom, the woman your husband slept with before you? Phew! You've married her, too. She can show up at the most surprising moments and you are expected to take the backseat and be cordial, regardless of whether she treats you like the live-in nanny or the town slut. And on top of that, you've learned it's just not practical to hate her.

Of course you're evil now and then!

My stepmother friend Stephanie will often call when she is at the end of her rope with her new family. A good Catholic girl, she is certain that she is going straight to hell because of the mean thoughts she has about her stepkids and their mother. One of her wildest fantasies is to pour salt on the ex-wife's well-manicured lawn in the middle of the night. She's so ashamed of herself that she tells me this in a whisper. I usually howl with laughter—such a sweet woman with such evil potential. I tell her not to chastise herself and to indulge me in more of her wicked stepmother fantasies. If you, too, fall into the black hole of evildom—and you will—remember two things. One, don't blame yourself for feeling the way you do. Two, find another stepmother friend to whom you can pour out your soul.

Sassy Stepmother Straight Scoop

There will be days, weeks, and months in your early days of stepmotherhood when you feel so wicked that you won't recognize yourself. Rest assured these evil thoughts are absolutely normal. I cringe when I think about the strange and unkind things I said to my husband about his kids and his ex-wife in those early days. (Thank God, Mark has a short memory.) I have since forgiven myself because I now understand that taking on a whole family complete with customs, traditions, and quirks that don't jibe with my own can be tricky and torturous at times.

Whose Honeymoon Is This Anyway?

Probably the most difficult concept I had to accept in my new role as wife and stepmother was the fact that my schedule, and more importantly my life, were no longer my own.

"I'm just not as free as I used to be," says Grace, a sassy stepmother from northern California. "No more hanging out at the gym, or Saturday afternoon movie marathons. Sometimes I get resentful about the ungodly amount of time we spend with the kids and the way their schedule impacts mine. I have so many more limitations on my life due to all these people: the kids, the ex-wife, the ex-wife's husband's ex-wife. It is one thing to share your life with one guy, but it is quite another to share it with a random group of people not of your choosing—particularly given the fact that up until a few years ago, the only beings I had to contend with on a daily basis were my coworkers, my friends, and my cats."

The first time the "my life is not my own" concept slapped me hard in the face was a few days before our wedding. While most soon-to-be brides spend their last hours before the wedding fretting about what they will wear on their wedding night (the white, frilly number or the whore getup complete with fishnets and a garter belt), I was negotiating how we would deal with our seven-year-old best man and three-year-old ring bearer after the wedding.

We had two choices. Either we could have Mark's ex-wife pick the boys up at the end of the wedding, or we could bring them home to our house for the night. While traditional wedding mythology had convinced me that there was only one way to spend a wedding night (alone together and naked), I opted instead to carry the sleeping ring bearer over our back-door threshold in my Vera Wang wedding dress, rather than share my day with my husband's ex-wife.

The next day Mark's exhausted sons stood on the front porch of our house with their grandmother, waving goodbye as we sped off to the airport. For our honeymoon we had decided to escape the gray, wet winter in Seattle for the sun and blue skies of Portugal. We both waved back from the window of the cab with mixed emotions. We were excited to get away, but sad to leave the boys behind.

I was surprised the following day when I stepped out of the warm hotel shower to find Mark on the phone. Naturally I leaned into the room and did my best to eavesdrop on the conversation. I was shocked to discover that he wasn't ordering up a plate of caviar and champagne, but instead treating his ex-wife to a verbal tour of Lisbon and outlining our itinerary. I silently fumed. "Isn't this my honeymoon? Isn't this my husband?" And so it went. We traveled, made mad passionate love, sipped port, and ate lots of cheese, and every four days Mark placed a call to his kids and his ex-wife.

I felt ripped off, like I had been forced to share my man and my honeymoon with another woman. My dashing knight was willing to compromise our romance in order to keep on good terms with his previous paramour. He hadn't prepared me for the fact that he expected to call his kids every few days, which would invariably include some cordial conversations with his ex-wife. When I pressed him on the issue he responded, "I didn't think it would matter." If it does matter to you, then I have some words of advice.

Manage Your Expectations with Your Man

First of all, remember, your politician husband has an incredibly difficult balancing act. He is trying to make sure all constituents are happy and unfortunately you are just one of many. Make yourself available to your husband as his partner and confidante, rather than one of many special interest groups he needs to please. Before a big weekend or a trip ask him about his expectations. "What do you want to do with the kids this weekend?" or "How often do you think we will be touching base with the kids on this vacation?" The more information you have about the family and your husband's obligations to them, the more in control and loved you will feel.

Regarding your honeymoon or any other intimate occasion, talk to your husband well in advance about how you envision the event. If you are set on being completely alone—sans telephone—be sure to let your husband know so he can apprise the ex-wife long before you embark on your romantic adventure. Trust me, the saying is true: Happy wife equals happy life. And that includes both wives, new and old.

You would probably prefer that your husband hate his ex-wife so he would never have to talk to her, or better yet that she didn't exist. In your heart of hearts you wish you could have been your husband's first wife and that your stepkids were your own. But that's not the way it is.

Instead of whining, thank your lucky stars that you found a great guy and a good father who is married to you—not his ex-wife. Be relieved that he works hard to keep in good standing with the kids' bio-mom—it's good for the kids and makes both your lives easier.

It's Not About You

I'll make this short because the concept is pretty basic. Now that you're married to your husband and the small village that comes along with him, your life is no longer all about you. I laugh hysterically at how self-centered I was when I first met my husband. It seemed everything his ex-wife did in the early days of our relationship somehow became, in my mind, a vicious conspiracy to unseat me.

When Jeanine, a young stepmother, first got married to her husband, Jack, she was certain that his ex-wife's decision to go back to school was based on a desire to compete with her, an MBA graduate. Jeanine had convinced herself that Jack's ex-wife was jealous of her and wanted to prove that she could be just as educated. What she never stopped to ponder was the possibility that Jack's ex might authentically be interested in higher education; after all, four painful years of school with a four-year-old at home is a steep price to pay in order to make an insignificant point. Now, several years later, Jack's ex-wife has her degree and is happily working as a business professional. And Jeanine, well, let's just say she was a little embarrassed when she realized that Jack's ex-wife's decision to go back to school had nothing to do with her.

Sassy Stepmother Straight Scoop

When you start to get paranoid or obsessed about being the target of a malicious and covert plot, bear in mind the fact that other people rarely think about you as much as you think about you. Be assured that your husband's ex-wife is thinking about a lot of things, namely herself and her kids. You, my dear, are way down on her list.

It Gets Better with Time

Not too long ago I was walking with my single friend Michelle, who at the time was dating a divorced guy with two teenage kids. On this particular day, Michelle's anger and frustration with her boyfriend's "impossible" schedule propelled us along at an Olympic pace. I could hardly keep up with her let alone carry on a conversation, not really such a problem since she was doing all the talking.

"I just can't take it," she said. "All of Steve's time is taken up by the kids or by his work. If I'm lucky, I get half a Friday night, and then he's absolutely worthless. I always have to work around his schedule, but he never works around mine. Very convenient for him, don't you think?"

She talked as if her boyfriend, Steve, who I happen to know is a kind and generous guy, was a selfish and stingy man, doling out rations of time and love at the apocalypse.

"I have had it! I'm just not going to be as available. Let's just see how he likes it when his schedule is no longer convenient for me," she huffed.

Michelle's insensitive "poor pitiful me" script was all too familiar. I remembered feeling as resentful and outraged years ago when I first got serious with my time-strapped man. But when Michelle voiced her irritation and anger aloud, I bristled. Now that I'd been through that experience, I couldn't imagine putting such high demands on a single dad with kids. She sounded more like a twelve-year-old, self-centered brat than the reasonable forty-four-year-old woman that I knew.

I had seen plenty of "perfect guys" traipse in and out of Michelle's life over our fifteen-year friendship, and I was certain that Steve, aside from all of his trappings, was truly the most "perfect guy" of them all. I worried that if she kicked him off the love bus, she would be back to dating the same commitment-phobic, workaholic, never-married guys. I tried to scare some sense into her by asking if she was prepared to go back to online dating again, but that didn't seem to have the snap-out-of-it effect I was hoping for.

Instead of listening to me, her wise stepmother confidante, she prattled on about how their split was imminent if things didn't change. Blah, blah, blah. It's too bad I didn't have a stepmother crystal ball for Michelle at the time. If I did, she would have seen that eventually the short-term "me, me, me" concerns that plagued her would eventually become trivial details in a much bigger, more important relationship. I wanted to shake her out of her anger spiral and tell her to quit being such a self-absorbed baby. But I didn't, and now Michelle is back to online dating without a decent prospect in sight. And Steve? Well, he's history.

Sassy Stepmother Straight Scoop

When you find that you would rather take a job along-side white-collar criminals cleaning up trash on the freeway than live another day sharing your man with his family, try to remember that you're in this for the long haul.

Stepmotherhood, like parenthood, is a personal journey. And while the road will seem downright im-passable at times, you will get to the other side a better and stronger person. It's easy for me to have this in-sight now, but back when I was first learning to live with my gaggle of guys, I thought the struggle and frus-trations would never end. So when you are ready to call it quits and hand over your stepmother badge, re-member these five simple words of advice: *It gets better with time!* Now, go tattoo that on your hand.

CHAPTER TWO

Embrace Your Identity Crisis

t this moment you may think you know who you are. You may even have a list of attributes on hand to describe yourself should someone ask—for example, successful business-woman, tennis buff, award show fanatic, retail enthusiast, romance novel addict, blah, blah, blah. Don't forget, you're also a new wife, or soon-to-be wife, of a man with children and an ex-wife. So go ahead—add "fledgling stepmother," "legitimate love slave," "Dad's new wife," and "chauffeur" to the list.

As you begin to embark upon the role of new wife and stepmommy, my guess is that you may become less sure of who and what you are. Don't worry—you're not losing your marbles. It's just a case of Stepmother Identity Crisis, aka SIC. My conversations with stepmothers across the country reveal that the single most annoying issue for a new stepmother, besides learning to share her life with people she doesn't know and may not even like, is surviving the unavoidable SIC. Like sagging breasts and menopause, there is no escaping it. However, with advance warning, the prepared stepmother can weather an otherwise difficult SIC with grace.

This Is Not My Beautiful Life!

Within the first trimester of stepmotherhood, my identity was in a shambles. Looking back, all I can say is, of course it was! If you are like me and married later than most, you probably had a single life that made your married-with-children friends envious and sitcom writers rich. My modus operandi when I was single was establishing a firm footing on the corporate ladder while avoiding mediocrity at all costs. I filled my life with culturally enriching events, athletic pursuits, and business travel. As far as my work associates and friends were concerned, I was a virtual concierge, always ready with the latest airline, hotel, theater, and restaurant recommendation.

In my downtime I devoured cooking magazines, Grisham novels, and anything Pulitzer. On weekends, when I wasn't hiking in the mountains with friends, I could be found strolling the halls of museums pondering the motivations of tortured artists or sitting in a vibrating chair at Top #1 Nails, having my toenails painted and catching up on the latest Hollywood gossip in *People* magazine. On Saturday nights, while the bourgeoisie and their kids waited in line at Blockbuster with a stack of the latest Disney films in their arms, I sat comfortably at the art house theater eating a dinner of unbuttered popcorn and a Diet Coke while watching intellectual indie films with subtitles. My Sunday morning routine, no less self-centered, included a power yoga class, a late brunch complete with Starbucks coffee, followed by an evening of *Seinfeld* reruns and a hydrating herbal face mask. It was the Sally Show—24-7, starring none other than me!

To say that life with kids and a husband was a contrast to my single life would be a colossal understatement. Words like *juvenile, tedious,* and *downright humdrum* come to mind. In the "fiancé" days of our relationship, I managed to escape the Elmo videos and the boys' petty arguments about who got the biggest bowl of Ben & Jerry's ice cream by feigning a work crisis or flying to the aid of a single girlfriend in need (with a bottle of wine at a swanky restaurant).

Transitioning Out of Your Single Life

After our wedding, however, things changed a bit. Obviously, my husband wanted me around more to be "part of the family," and I felt a little guilty leaving him alone with the kids while I was out on the town. So I went cold turkey. I traded in my old life for a spot on our couch in the basement, where I watched, with my new family, endless games of baseball while sipping Gatorade and eating plates of homemade nachos.

I felt like I was wasting my life. The very thought of sitting at home with a napping child on a sunny Saturday afternoon while my friends were out biking in the San Juan Islands made me hyperventilate. And forget about trying to get a seven-year-old boy to play "spa" with me. The boys had no interest in the art of exfoliation and screamed when I opened a bottle of nail polish remover. Instead of enjoying amateur aesthetician nights at home, I was reduced to building spaceships of LEGOs and munching on Cheetos while the rest of the world took in live music and danced their tails off.

Seven months into my marriage I was distraught and in desperate need of a "single life" booster shot, or at the very least a girl's month out. There was nothing about my new life that resembled my old one. I struggled to hold on to my identity while I was sucked into my new role and family.

When my friend Jackie tied the knot with her tall, strapping fireman and his litter of three kidlets, she practically threw her old life and friends under the bus. I know—I was one of them. Within minutes of walking down the proverbial aisle, she ditched her book club of nine years, stopped working out at the gym, and completely gave up on returning phone calls. I was getting ready to file a missing person's report with the local authorities when I bumped into her at the local market buying groceries for a newfangled gourmet concoction she had discovered in a fancy-pansy cooking magazine (Jackie didn't and doesn't cook). In an effort to get a limb on her new family tree, Jackie immersed herself in the Evelyn Wood School of Speed Stepparenting. She basically stopped doing the things she loved to do and started doing the things her husband and his kids loved to do. In the end she got so grumpy and resentful she hardly recognized herself and neither did her new husband. After a rough SIC that had her rethinking her marriage vows, Jackie finally went along with her husband to see a marriage counselor. Jackie was diagnosed with posttraumatic stepparent syndrome and was cautioned to take a more gradual approach to her transition from single girl to wedded woman. She has since given up her Julia Child impersonation and reclaimed her old self. She is now, thank God, back to the oven-phobic woman her husband (and his kids) originally married.

Sassy Stepmother Straight Scoop

I know from watching many of my friends that moving from sassy and single to happy and hitched can be a rough transition by itself—throw in kids and an ex-wife and you have a recipe for a domestic crisis that rivals Monicagate. If you're like me and have lived your single life by the mantra "My way or the highway," you may find making nice with the ex-wife, chipping in for child support, and cleaning up the vomit of a child who is not your own particularly challenging.

Do I recommend stepmotherhood? Absolutely! But words to the wise: Don't do what many women do and go cold turkey on your single life. Instead give yourself some time to get used to your new identity as a wife and part-time mother. Most stepmothers I talked to, bless their pleasing hearts, did not give themselves the proper time to acclimate to their new lives with kids and a husband. Instead, they enthusiastically jumped in headfirst without looking back, only to discover months later, amid anger and resentment, that in their quest to become the perfect wife and stepmother, they had become mere shells of their old selves and snapping turtles to those they love.

Remember, "until death do you part" is a very long time. Your husband isn't going to pack his bags and leave a good-bye note on the counter if it takes a while for you to get comfortable sitting at home and eating hot dogs and Oreos on Friday nights. Instead of turning your back on your old life, learn to weave in the old activities with the new. For example, instead of committing to an entire season of Little League games or gymnastics meets, negotiate with your husband to attend one out of every three. That way you'll ease gracefully into your life as a stepmother while maintaining some of your independence.

Identity Theft—Making Friends with Your Evil Twin

Unfortunately stepmotherhood brings out the best and the worst in a woman, and unlike regular marriages sans kids, it does so right out of the gates. Enter the Evil Twin. You know her. She arrives unannounced, saying nasty things and convincing you to act in ways that you're sure to regret in the morning. You'd like to dismiss her actions by telling your family and friends, "That mean girl last night? I know you thought she was me, but it wasn't. That was my Evil Twin." Evil Twins are not aspects of ourselves that we're proud of. In fact, many stepmothers would do an across-the-board Evil Twin trade-in for a bad case of PMS or a life full of conspicuous panty lines. But like PMS, she's not so easy to get rid of.

My friend Maryann says, "It's like *Invasion of the Body Snatchers.* When my husband and his kids push my buttons, I get possessed by this very unlikable prepubescent little brat, screaming and yelling as if it's the end of the world. I clench my hands and grit my teeth and say to my husband, 'I can't take it anymore!' At the time my unseemly outburst feels great. But when it's over I'm completely shamed."

I know exactly where Maryann is coming from. One day, I had spent an afternoon slaving over the stove in an effort to create the "perfect meal" for my family. I was worn-out and still perspiring from hours in the kitchen, and the last thing I expected to hear at the dinner table was a seven-year-old boy whine, "Yuck, you know I don't like this" (stepmother translation: "Your cooking stinks, and so do you"). Poof! Just like Clark Kent I transformed into Superevil Twin just in time to set him straight. "Listen, you're darn lucky to be eating at all, mister. May I remind you that you are not my child and with behavior like that I'd just as soon see you starve!" Incensed by his behavior, my Evil Twin got up from the table, threw her napkin at her husband, and stormed into the kitchen, where she proceeded to throw utensils in the sink, slam several drawers, and curse under her breath (I just hate it when she acts like that!). Afterward her steely silence had the family so scared they sat like expressionless mannequins in their seats. I watched them staring at her and all I could think was "I wish I could push the rewind button and start all over because I feel like an idiot."

My stepmommy friend Carrie has a name for her Evil Twin; she calls her Brett the Brat and is known to regale me with stories of her delinquent behavior. While I howl with laughter at Carrie's outrageous tales of Brett, I know in my heart that her family doesn't find them nearly as amusing, nor does she.

But the Evil Twin is not entirely bad. She's there to fend off the enemy when you're feeling threatened or scared. I like to think of mine as a veritable gauge of household juju. Punctual and protective, she shows up on the doorstep of my brain like an aggressive Girl Scout selling boxes of rage just as I'm starting to feel alienated by my family, taken for granted by my stepchildren, or just plain powerless in the face of it all (common feelings in the infant stage of stepmotherhood).

Sassy Stepmother Straight Scoop

Let's face it: Jumping into a family with kids and an ex-wife is like being dropped into the jungles of the Amazon in strappy heels and a sundress without sunscreen, a map, or bug repellent. No wonder you're more at home in your Evil Twin's skin than your own. But no matter how out of sorts you feel in your new role as stepmother and wife, your Evil Twin must be tamed. If not, you will be destined to a life of self-loathing and/or divorce.

Having exposed my borderline personality to my very confused husband and his kids one too many times, I finally learned to tame my Evil Twin. Now at the first trace of my unwanted houseguest, I try to stop, take a deep breath, and think specifically about why I'm feeling so perturbed. Once I identify the actions that are pushing my buttons (bad manners, disrespect, snotty attitude, loneliness), I am better able to sit down calmly and address the real problem with my husband and family. I have also learned (the hard way) to bite my tongue when I have the urge to make a sweeping, derogatory statement about the bunch of them. Instead, I try to stick to the subject at hand, rather than let my Evil Twin indict our family and our marriage. Sounds very simple, doesn't it? Well, it isn't. Getting calm is an art form. One of the ways I have learned to pacify myself in the heat of the moment is to chant my very own mantra. It goes something like this:

I am a grown-up.
I am a good person.
This is not about me.

I am a grown-up.
I am a good person.
This is not about me.

I am a grown-up.
I am a good person.
This is not about me.

> Eventually, if I chant long enough, my heart calms to a reasonable pace and I am able to see the situation for what it is.
>
> My friend Jackie believes that prudent planning is the only way to fend off the Evil Twin. Every other Tuesday she and her husband have a strategic planning meeting "off-site" (usually at a restaurant over steak and wine), where they plot with Franklin Covey precision their upcoming weekend with the kids. Along with schedule planning, they discuss expectations, anxieties, and desires regarding their time with the kids. Having prepared ahead of time, Jackie and her husband go into the weekend aware of potential "land mines" and better equipped to sidestep them.

The Mommy Club—No Stepmothers Allowed!

Just when you thought you'd gotten your Evil Twin in check, you discover that there is yet another stepmother annoyance ahead called the Mommy Club. If you haven't discovered it yet, you will. It's an exclusive society, a sorority of sorts, that you will encounter in your first few months and years of stepmotherhood. Sadly, you will not be invited unless you biologically spawn, carry, and give birth to a child of your own (vaginal or cesarean delivery will do). An exception to the rule is occasionally made for those women who cannot give birth and therefore go through the bureaucratic labor of adoption. The good news is, once you're in the club, you cannot be thrown out. The bad news is, if you're not in it—you're out of it.

My friend Jane was dumbfounded when, after attending ballet classes for three months, she let it slip that she was Tina's stepmother. "By the looks on the faces of the other mothers you would have thought I had confessed to kidnapping her at a Wal-Mart parking lot," says Jane. " 'I thought for sure you were her mother,' one of the women chimed in a disappointed voice. After that, I was never treated with quite the same hospitality as I had been when they thought I was my stepdaughter's bio-mom."

I first encountered the Mommy Club when I began attending my stepson's Little League games. I cheered enthusiastically from the bleachers for my stepson ("You go get 'em, Guy!"). My fervor was no less authentic than that of most of the mothers who hooted and hollered around me. "Which one's yours?" asked a woman sitting next to me. When I pointed to my stepson on the field, my assertion was met with the usual confusion.

"Guy's yours? I thought he was . . ."

I staved off the potential befuddlement with the confession, "Well, he's not actually mine. He's my stepson."

"Oh, OK, I get it," she said, putting it all together in her head.

Compelled to clear things up for the stranger beside me, I pointed out Guy's bio-mom a few feet over on the bleachers—the two of them exchanged hellos and that was the end of my short friendship with the third baseman's mother. I guess she would rather befriend the real deal than a weekend warrior.

During the first few months of my Little League initia-
tion, I watched the bio-moms bond like superglue. They
shared stories about their jobs, grumbled about the um-
pire's bad calls, traded play dates, and arranged car pools
among themselves. No one asked me what I did for a living
or acknowledged that I was a part-time parent. Even though
I transported the kids from school to the baseball field and
made their dinner when they returned from the game, the
other mothers didn't seem to take me seriously. I felt like a
drag queen in a sea of women—almost but not quite the real
deal. I wanted to paste a sign on my back that said "Hey, I'm
not the home wrecker you think I am! He was divorced
when we met. I'm just a girl trying to make my way!"

As uncomfortable as it was making small talk with people
who barely acknowledged my existence, I hung in there hoping that the mothers around me would eventually include
me. I had always been a girl's girl and thought that it was just
a matter of time before they found me to be delightful and
deserving of their friendships. Not so. My awkward conversations with moms on the bleachers and in school hallways
fell flat, leaving me to wonder, "What did I say?" I tried to
strike up conversations about work, about family, about politics. I verbally praised the skills of other children and mem-
orized the names of all the kids on the team. The more I
prattled on, the more dubious my role seemed.

It didn't help that most of the conversations I initiated
with other mothers were about the things I knew best, like
my favorite celebrity couple, a new movie release, or a
mod restaurant opening in a foreign city. Most of their
"real mom" conversations, on the other hand, ended up
being about topics I had no knowledge of or interest in,

like school levies, entrance exams for private junior highs, and childhood food allergies. I found myself scrambling to sound intelligent, but the subject just kept coming back to the topic I knew best—popular culture. After all, I had just come from fifteen years of a blissfully child-free, all-about-me existence.

No matter how hard I tried, I couldn't conjugate mommy talk and I wasn't about to fake it. So I kept my mouth shut on subjects I knew nothing about and hung on to my husband like arm candy as he discussed the varying school board autocracies and the merits of a public pre-school education versus a private one.

In the end, I found the impenetrable Mommy Club to be a tight group of women devoted to their own kind. It seems the unspoken law among Mommy Club members is that bio-moms, whatever the case, reign. It's a girl thing. I think on some level, happily married women are threatened by stepmothers because it absolutely breaks their heart to contemplate handing their children and husband off to another woman. I suspect they believe opening their heart to a stepmother somehow condones divorce or infidelity, even though many stepmothers, like me, married their husbands long after the men were divorced from their first wives. Mothers I have gotten to know over the years do accept me, but they do not respect me in the same way they do the kids' bio-mom. In the Mommy Club such treachery is not allowed.

My hilarious and fabulous friend Lorna told me one day over a lunch of sushi and sake that her remedy for being excluded from the Mommy Club is to lie. "Sometimes I just get tired of being on the outside. I want in on the inside track. So if the opportunity arises and Ryan [her stepson] is out of earshot, I just pretend that he's mine. If someone says, 'Your son is so cute and smart,' I say, 'Oh, thank you, he's been like that since he was in the womb.' I love the respect I get when people think he's my blood. I guess you could say it's weird that I like to lie like that," she adds sheepishly, "but it's fun to see how the other half lives."

Sassy Stepmother Straight Scoop

Here are the facts. You need to accept the reality that you will not, under any circumstances, be admitted into the Mommy Club (unless of course you bear children), so do not let it damage your self-esteem or impact your identity. Your exclusion is not about you or your ability to truly love your stepkid(s); it is about bio-moms feeling threatened and their need to keep the club homogenous. As long as you share important events like ball games, piano recitals, or graduations with your stepkid's mother, you will not be considered a real parent by anyone. It's something you'll have to live with.

After many years of unrequited gestures of friendship I have learned to attend my stepchildren's extracurricular events with an ego-free attitude and a solid sense of myself. I have finally come to grips with the fact that I am not at these events because I want to be popular or liked by the other parents. I am there, instead, to show support for my stepson.

If I'm Not Their Mother, Then Who Am I?

One night my friend Ava was out with her husband and his two children, eating greasy burgers and fries at a neighborhood restaurant, when her seven-year-old stepdaughter decided to put her smack-dab in her place. She said with a condescending tone reserved for nerds on the playground, "Ava, you're nice and stuff, but you're nobody's mother!" She may as well have said, "You're an ugly slut and a nobody." Ava was devastated. Her husband gave her an apologetic smile and without missing a beat, he and his children went back to eating their fries and soda.

Ava sat staring at the three of them, wondering how to take this hurtful yet accurate statement. It felt more like a punch in the stomach than a comment on her maternal history. Her stepdaughter was right, though; technically she was nobody's mother—namely the child's. No matter how hard Ava tried, she hadn't fooled her into thinking that she had the skills or the background to claim "real motherhood."

"I wanted to say, 'Yeah, well, maybe I'm not a mom, but I'm a good employee.' Thank God I stopped myself because I am sure she would have looked at me as if I were some crazy fool," says Ava. "In a little seven-year-old girl's world there are no workers. Instead there are mommies and daddies and kids—nothing else."

So if Ava wasn't a mom, and her other life outside her family didn't seem to matter to the forty-pound know-it-all, what was she, then? Chopped liver? A nice waitress? A cleaning lady? Ava left the diner that night feeling small and lost. Her new, well-constructed identity as a mother figure was shattered simply because her stepdaughter was trying to set the record straight for herself.

Sassy Stepmother Straight Scoop

Your kids will say things along the way that will require you to be as strong a person as you have ever been. They can sniff out insecurity and fear far better than any adult you know. It will be important that when they question your role or threaten your importance in the family, you stay strong and self-confident. With a smile make statements like "Yes, you're right—I am nobody's mother technically. But that's good news for you, miss, because it gives me more time to be an evil stepmother to you!" Confidence goes a long way with kids. The stronger you are in your role as a stepmother, the more respect you will get from them. So try to be very sure of yourself, even if you have to fake it.

Hey, Wait a Second—Is That the Ex-Wife in the Refrigerator?

Establishing your own identity as a new wife and stepmother is hard enough without the constant reminder that your husband's ex-wife is never more than a phone call away. There will be times when you'll swear she's on your back, in the woodwork, or—worse—in your refrigerator.

All of my friends know that I hate rice milk, and soy milk, too. At my very core, I am a cow's-milk kind of girl—organic of course. What can I say? I'm the grand-daughter of a dairy farmer. Milk from any other thing, plant or beast, in my opinion, is not really milk.

My husband's ex-wife, on the other hand, doesn't have the same emotional attachment to cow's milk that I do and instead prefers rice milk in her household. When Mark and I first moved in together, the boys let me know in no uncertain terms that they disapproved of my milk choice with their signature "Euuuuhhhhh! Cow's milk. Yucky! We don't drink cow's milk at my mom's house!"

At first this holier-than-thou, anti-cow's-milk attitude made me fume with disgust. It felt so . . . so . . . politi-cal. When I suggested a cow's-milk substitute the boys put on their best Shakespeare imitation and writhed like Romeo on the kitchen floor as if I were offering up the grocery store equivalent of cyanide. But their high-and-mighty anti-cow's-milk logic didn't seem to jibe with the fact that Ben & Jerry's was their favorite after-dinner snack and hot cocoa with whipped cream was a Saturday ritual.

I was incensed that in an effort to establish my new identity as a wife and mother I would not only have to ad-just to my husband's addiction to ESPN but I would also have to adapt to the nonsensical whims of his people, in-cluding his ex-wife.

But the thing that really killed me about having rice milk in my fridge, tucked between the two percent and the half-and-half, was that in some insidious way it meant that not only was my husband's ex-wife in our lives, but she was in our refrigerator, too.

Furthermore I was besotted with guilt. Every time I threw a box of rice milk in the grocery cart and covered it up with bags of pretzels and chips, I felt like the Benedict Arnold of my dairy-farming family. I could hear my udder-squeezing grandfather and fresh-ice-cream-making grandmother groan in their graves as I poured the thin filmy white liquid over a bowl of raisin bran for my stepson.

Sassy Stepmother Straight Scoop

There will be times early on in your marriage when you will swear the ex-wife is a monkey on your back pressuring you to buy things or do things that are contradictory to your value system. While these purchases or actions may make you cringe, keep in mind you are marrying a family that existed long before you arrived on the scene. Your mission will be to learn to adapt to all these individuals with their quirks and whims while maintaining your own values and ideals. It is not a question of who is right or who is wrong but rather an appreciation for different ways of being.

So when your stepchildren criticize your ways of doing things, try not to let it get under your skin. Instead remember to hold your tongue and count to a million. When you're done counting, you will have forgotten what it was that made you so mad in the first place.

Role Models Wanted

The fact that there are no high-profile stepmother role models in the media doesn't help when you're trying to form your new identity as a wife and pseudomother. (Hello, television executives—who do you think is remarrying the increasing number of divorcées?) In fact, there have been only a handful of attempts on the part of the entertainment industry to portray a stepmother, and the fictional stepmothers that have been created are a far cry from the real thing.

Several years ago Columbia Pictures released the much hyped movie *Stepmom*, starring Julia Roberts. After reruns of old-fashioned parenting models, i.e., Carol Brady, Eddie's father, and Mr. French, I was relieved to finally have a modern tale about a not-so-nuclear family.

Aside from the great fashions, beautiful cinematography, and star-studded cast, the movie was a disaster. Long-term family conflicts between the stepmother and the bio-mom in the story were carefully alleviated as the writers jettisoned the bio-mom (Susan Sarandon) from the family by giving her terminal cancer. In the end, Roberts's character rides off into the sunset with her new family—the ex-wife permanently out of the picture. As an inexperienced stepmother, I was hoping that the movie might provide some inspiration for my new role; instead it made me think that the formula for successful stepmotherhood was a case of terminal cancer.

Sassy Stepmother Straight Scoop

Save yourself the trip to the video store because there are no how-to videos, no stepmother Lamaze courses, and no authoritative Miss Manners manual to outline the proper protocol for bridging your old single-girl identity with your new stepmother identity. So here's what I suggest you do: Look for other stepmothers out there to talk to. Many of the most insightful and therapeutic discussions I have had on the subject of step-parenting have been with other stepmothers. Our chats have revealed that I am not alone in my frustrations with being a part-time mother and a new wife.

A Woman Without a Country

OK, so I just told you that you're definitely going to have some kind of identity crisis; the moms of the Mommy Club are going to reject you; your Evil Twin, if she hasn't arrived yet, is on her way; and you have absolutely no stepmother role models to follow. So where does that put you? Well, in terms of creating your new identity, it puts you smack-dab in the middle of no-woman's-land. Does that mean that you are destined to sit on the back bench at T-ball games or at a wobbly desk with only three legs in the classroom at Parents' Night? Absolutely not. Here are your choices, my dear: You can either be reduced to a whiny withering stepmother or garner the appreciation and admiration you deserve by standing up for yourself and be-coming a strong and proud stepmother. You decide.

One early morning, my stepmother friend Debbie's oldest stepson woke up sick. Her husband and the child's bio-mom had work conflicts that could not budge, so Debbie, having just come off an intense work cycle at her ad agency job, volunteered to forfeit a day at the office in order to try her hand at nurturing. When her husband left for work that morning, she enthusiastically put on her best Florence Nightingale impersonation and mollycod-dled her snotty-nosed stepson. It was fun. They watched television, ate Jell O, and played Chutes and Ladders. Later, when Debbie called in to work to apprise her boss of the situation, she was shocked to hear her otherwise flexible boss's reaction to the news that she would not be in the office that day.

"Sick with a kid? You don't have kids," the senior manager said. While she herself was a mother and was well aware of Debbie's stepparent status, she did not give Deb-bie the same respect she would have given her bio-mom employees.

When Debbie hung up she wondered, "If I'm not a parent, what am I? A free babysitter?" The dismissive telephone exchange left Debbie feeling stung. Was staying home with a child she had not given birth to the equiva-lent of playing hooky?

The very next day, after beefing and stewing on the meaty subject of who really has the right to stay home with a sick child, Debbie decided to go directly to her insensi-tive boss and tell her exactly how she felt about their con-versation from the previous day. She calmly told her that she did not appreciate the fact that her parenting role was put into question and asked that in the future her boss show her more respect for her not-so-unique family situation. Debbie's boss sheepishly responded with a look of surprise and then thanked Debbie for her straightforward approach. She never questioned whether or not Debbie was a parent again.

Sassy Stepmother Straight Scoop

For a stepmother, no-woman's-land is a tough place to be, largely because it is entirely up to you to create your identity. Unlike in other professions or roles in life, there are no clear expectations or guidelines for stepmothers. It's up to you to create them for yourself. And once you do, you need to state your position loud and clear. Sometimes you may feel like a very squeaky wheel or a broken record, but remember, the more you remind people about the importance of your role, the sooner you will be given the respect you deserve.

While carving out your place in your ready-made family is not easy, establishing your new identity as a stepmother and wife is even more difficult, so cut yourself some slack as you move from your old life to your new one and be prepared to go through a bit of an SIC. And while you're moving into your new role as a wife and stepmommy, take some time to think about the woman you are and the stepmother you'd like to be. Remember, the choice is yours; no one is going to tell you who you should become or how to act. Be assured that in time you will be able to stand proudly and make the claim, "See that kid over there—she's mine. I'm her stepmother and I'm damn proud of it!"

I laugh looking back at my life over the past few years, amazed at how much I have changed. There was a time when I could not be indoors for more than two hours without going nuts. Now, seven years later, there is nothing I enjoy more than sitting around the living room table playing Concentration or cracking jokes with my stepsons. But it didn't happen overnight. It took me a few years to understand that building sand castles, hunting for geckos, or playing charades with children can be more stimulating and intellectually challenging than watching a foreign film and eating popcorn for dinner. Who knew?

CHAPTER THREE

Bonding with a Kid Who's Bound to Break Your Heart

When I first got married I used to say to my husband, "All right, now, let me see if I have this straight: It was you and your ex-wife who got divorced, right? I was just going along minding my own business when you and your kids showed up on the scene. And without much arm-twisting, I fell in love and enthusiastically agreed to help raise, love, shuttle, and financially support your children. And now, come to find out, they're mean to me. Explain that!"

Save your husband the same unnecessary and seemingly unanswerable question and allow me to explain it to you firsthand. Bottom line, your stepkids are going to break your heart at least 10.5 times a month during your first few years of stepmotherhood. This highly scientific projection is based on stepmothers who see their stepkids on a semiweekly basis. If you're a summertime and holiday stepmom and see your stepkids for longer stretches of time but less frequently, you should be prepared to have your heart broken about, well, hmmmm, let's say every few minutes. But rest assured, as with an inevitable bad hair day, you'll get used to it. Eventually you will grow calluses on your delicate heart, and things that used to make you drown in tears will roll right off you like a distasteful joke. I wish for all the new stepmothers out there that it didn't have to be this way, but it is, so you might as well just buck up and get used to it!

The Crazy Things Kids Say

In my six-year tenure as a stepmother I have been spit on, lied to, scoffed at, ignored, and purposely tripped. I have been told that I'm nobody's favorite, nobody's mother, and most importantly "nobody's boss." I am still told that I am weird, crazy, and strange (which I now consider a compliment). I have been given unusual nicknames such as Salavana, Salary (celery), and simply Salad. I have survived embarrassing moments when the kids ask their dad outrageous questions in my company such as "Dad, when are you going to divorce Sally?" or "Dad, why can't you come live at Mom's house?" I'm finally at the point where it takes more than shocking comments, name-calling, and rolling eyes to offend me. I've learned to hold my tears and my tongue and to keep my cool when what the little darlings say infuriates me or makes me want to cry.

Sassy Stepmother Straight Scoop

As a stepmother you must learn to accept the fact that kids aren't always really sure what they're saying. Usually what comes tumbling out of their mouths is cute and charming, but when it's vicious, mean-spirited, and directed at you, it can be downright distressing. And while sometimes it seems like your stepkids are intentionally trying to push your buttons, often they have no clue about the hurtful impact of their words or actions. After all, they're just kids, and like you they're trying to figure out who's on first in this new family configuration. My stepmother friend Cheryl gives this advice: "In the first couple years, take everything your stepkids say with a grain of salt and don't let it get to you. Don't expect much from them—they're as confused as you are, if not more."

One caveat on this topic. If your stepchild blatantly disrespects you, calls you names, or verbally abuses you, taking it with a grain of salt simply won't do. If you find yourself in such an unsavory position, do not engage in a verbal battle with your stepchild. Instead simply tell him/her that you will not tolerate such inappropriate behavior, and then walk away, hand it over to the biologicals, and/or seek professional help. End of story.

You're Not My Mother— I Love You Not!

Remember the daisy game? The one you used to play with your girlfriends in the school yard that left your fingers stained with daisy juice? I don't know the exact history of the game, but it seems to me it was an old-fashioned Mother Nature tarot reading that determined if your paramour loved you or loved you not. Figuring out where you stand in your stepchildren's hearts is not unlike the daisy game. Some days they love you and on others they love you not. In the case of your stepkids, however, there is a lot less hocus-pocus in determining whether you're adored or abhorred. Unlike a school yard crush, they'll come right out and give it to you straight—regardless of what the daisy tells you.

When my youngest stepson was three years old, I had the duty of picking him up at his little French preschool every Tuesday at five p.m. It was the highlight of my week. Gavin, the perfect audience, sat captivated in his car seat behind me while I serenaded him with a repertoire of show tunes à la Bette Midler. It was a great arrangement: I sang my heart out and he howled with laughter. Those fun-filled rides home were like minivacations that left me feeling refreshed and inspired. And while I never totally forgot that I wasn't his mother, there were Tuesdays with Gavin when we had so much fun together I couldn't help but imagine how great it would be if I were. Thanks to Gavin, my delusions of motherhood were fleeting.

One winter evening I arrived at Gavin's school a little

early. It was sunny outside, which has the same effect on Seattleites in winter as catnip does on cats. The kids were taking advantage of the sunny weather, running around the school yard like gerbils in their Habitrail. With a sneaky smile on my face, I walked up to the gate outside hoping to surprise Gavin. As I reached over to unlatch the gate, one of his little preschool mates spotted me and blew my cover. He yelled to Gavin, "Hey, Gavin, your mom's here." Gavin spun around quickly and when he saw me he frowned. Then he turned to his friend on the playground and belted out a red-faced, fist-clenched, curdling scream: "She's not my mother!" The playground froze. The French teacher and her gaggle of three-year-old munchkins stared at me as if I were the Wicked Witch from Oz or at the very least a kidnapper. Speechless and surprised that my show tune buddy had demoted me to the role of pathetic understudy, I decided to get on my knees and tie my shoe (this gave me some time to gather my wits after the three year-old's tongue lashing). When I stood up, however, I was surprised to see Gavin at my side with his green froggie backpack in hand rarin' to go. He looked up at me, said "Hi, Sally," and grabbed my hand. When we got to the gate he yelled over his shoulder to his teacher, "Bye-bye, Marie Joelle." We walked up the hill to my car as he babbled on about his new Buzz Lightyear toy he had left at his mom's house. "I can't wait to show it to you! It's so cool."

I drove home from the École française that day a little changed. Gavin's need to violently clear up his family tree with his preschool cronies left me wounded and wondering, "Am I that bad?" It took me a while to learn that what he really meant to say to the oblivious kid was, "You dummy, you know that's not my mother. My mother picks me up almost every day and she has brown hair. That's Sally—clearly you can see she does not have brown hair, so of course she's not my mother." Now, years later, when my kids say something akin to "You're not my mother," I give it right back to them and say, "Well, duh, you're not my son."

Sassy Stepmother Straight Scoop

All the books I have read about stepparenting advise that when it comes to loving and parenting your stepchildren you should be mindful of the fact that you are not their biological parent. When I first read this warning, I imagined memory-challenged stepparents across America posting sticky notes on refrigerators and bathroom mirrors. "Don't forget to get milk, renew the car tabs, do the laundry, oh, and by the way, remember, you're not her mother." Were stepparents generally dim-witted? I wondered. Surely a detail of this magnitude could not be easily forgotten. Could it?

There will be times when you'll swear you're madly in love with your husband's child. In a sentimental split second when you're laughing hysterically at a new joke he learned at school, or you're bouncing the bundle of joy who smells like a mix of fresh mowed grass and stinky feet on your lap, you will wish he were your own. You may even go as far as to claim to a stranger (behind his/her back of course) that the child is your flesh and blood.

If this typical tug-of-heart amnesia befalls you, do not despair; you are not insane or on the verge of running off to Disneyland with your stepchild. It's natural to fall head over heels in love with the child of your spouse. But bear in mind, playground studies reveal that kids across the nation believe one mother is enough. So don't try to pull the wool over anyone's eyes, especially your own. Even if you do, your stepchild is likely to set the record straight with a "You're not my mother!" that is sure to break your heart (at least the first time).

Be assured that your stepkids will always be there to remind you, just in case you suffer a brief memory loss, that you cannot, in any uncertain terms, hold a candle to their mother. And if that's not bad enough, they have no reservations about adding salt to the wound with the authoritative and heated reprimand "And don't you forget it!"

I find that humor is a good buffer when my feelings get hurt by my stepsons. When they verbally reject me with something akin to "Ehhhhh, don't hug me," I give it right back to them with "What are you, crazy? I wasn't going to hug you—I was going to bop you on the head." And then I follow through by bopping them lightly on the head and we all laugh.

My Mom Doesn't Do It That Way

Just when you start to think you have your stepmother legs under you, the cute little critic known as your stepchild is bound to knock you off-balance with the all-knowing statement "My mom doesn't do it that way." Don't be surprised if you begin to feel like you have one of those obnoxious talking parrots on your shoulder reminding you every time you make pancakes or read bedtime stories that your way is not quite the right way (his or her mom's way).

My friend Jessica, a stepmother of two preteen stepdaughters, says that early on her girls pulled the "My mom doesn't do it that way" routine so many times that she began to wonder if their mother had embedded time-released microchips in their brains designed to drive her crazy. "It got to the point where I could see it coming. Chloe, who was only six at the time, would scrunch up her face and then shake her head slowly and say, 'That's not how my mom does it.' "

Darcy, a stepmother and career woman, is continually haunted by her husband's Happy Homemaker ex-wife. To say that her domestic skills pale in comparison to those of her husband's ex would be a gross understatement, and her seven- and eight-year-old stepkids are forever reminding her of that. One Saturday morning, on a whim, Darcy decided to show off some cooking flair by whipping up an impromptu batch of pancakes for her family. The breakfast was for all intents and purposes a big success until her youngest stepdaughter, who had snarfed down six cakes, remarked, "My mom makes pancakes in the shape of Mickey Mouse's head." Darcy snapped back, "Well, good for your mom. But around here I make pancakes in the shape of full moons."

Sassy Stepmother Straight Scoop

Even if you don't have a competitive bone in your body, you will begin to feel like you're in a contest for Mommy of the Year when your stepchildren start critiquing your every move with their signature "My mom doesn't do it that way." As aggravating and annoying as it may sound, be assured that this "Mom's way or the highway" thing has nothing to do with you. It is simply a reminder that you will never be able to replace their mother.

Most stepmothers I know want nothing more than to be the antithesis of their husbands' ex-wives, but that's not something I suggest you share with the kids. You may even be tempted in stressful moments to snap back, "If I did everything your mom did, I'd be divorced!" But don't do that, because your stepchild is guaranteed to share your snide remark with her mother. The best way to handle "My mom doesn't do it that way" is to say something diplomatic such as "Your mother's way sounds like a good way for her. My way, however, works better for me."

You're Nobody's Favorite—Come Here, Come Here, Get Away, Get Away

Marti, a stepmother of three girls, remembers one afternoon early on in her marriage when her heart was nearly destroyed by her ten-year-old stepdaughter, Jade.

In an attempt to bond with her new stepdaughter, Marti had offered to take Jade to Frenchy's, the local day spa, for an afternoon of pampering and lunch. Jade, a girlie girl with a penchant for pink, was delighted. When they got there, the receptionist sat Marti and Jade right next to each other in matching pink chairs. They flipped through magazines and sipped lemonade and decaffeinated tea while the manicurists buffed and polished their nails. Women in the chairs beside theirs engaged Jade in conversation and smiled at Marti as if she were Jade's mother. An older woman who was also getting a pedicure reached over and touched Jade's arm and said, "You have a nice mother. Apparently she is teaching you the value of pampering." Jade smiled back, nodding enthusiastically. When their afternoon of buffing and polishing was done, Jade and Marti walked out to the car hand in hand. Marti gave herself an imaginary pat on the back—obviously her strategy was working.

Later that night after Marti and Jade returned home, Jade asked her dad if she could call her mother. Marti overheard the conversation as the excited ten-year-old regaled her mom with highlights of the afternoon.

When it came time to tuck Jade into bed, Marti

sat down beside her. "I had so much fun today, Jade."

Jade smiled somewhat sheepishly and nodded, looking down at her hands. "Me, too." Marti noticed that Jade's mood had changed substantially since her phone conversation with her mother.

"Is something wrong, honey?" Marti asked.

"I miss my mom."

"You'll see her tomorrow," Marti comforted.

"I know, but I miss her," Jade said, avoiding eye contact with Marti by pretending to admire her fingernails. "Marti, you know you're not my favorite."

"What?" Marti said, not sure if she had heard her correctly.

"You're not my favorite," Jade repeated.

Marti's heart ached. She felt like she was back in third grade getting dumped by her best friend.

"Honey," she said, choking back her tears, "I know I'm not your favorite. How could I be? Your daddy and your mommy are your favorites."

With that, Jade sat up in bed and gave Marti a big, long bear hug. Marti realized then that by acknowledging and accepting Jade's version of the family pecking order, she had earned invaluable points as a stepmother.

Sassy Stepmother Straight Scoop

No relationship is more sacred than that of mother and child. As you begin to bond with your stepchild, you may find that he becomes emotionally confused about how to divvy up his love and loyalty for his bio-mom and you, his stepmother. No matter how much fun the two of you have together, it is highly likely that if forced to make a choice, your stepchild will voluntarily throw you under the bus in order to prove his loyalty to his bio-mom. Save your sanity and a broken heart by repeating the mantra "It's not about me."

The Unrequited Wave

It's one thing to get your feelings hurt by your stepchildren in the comfort of your own home, but it is quite another when you're in an unfamiliar location in the presence of acquaintances, strangers, and your husband's ex-wife. My first public humiliation and rejection as a stepmother occurred with the notorious "unrequited wave." I am not alone in this, as many stepmothers I know have been guilty of enthusiastically waving themselves into oblivion.

Typically the unrequited wave happens in a crowd at a school function or a sporting event. You're one of the many proud fans showing your support for your husband's budding prodigy, and just when your stepchild completes Mozart's Fifth on the piano, catches the winning fly ball, or wins first place for his newfangled science project, you jump enthusiastically to your feet, waving and cheering like a twelve-year-old girl at her first Christina Aguilera concert. Your stepson, equally pleased with his performance, smiles and looks out into the crowd; he catches your eye and looks away; then he waves back—to his mother. You're sure he must not have seen you—otherwise he would have acknowledged you. So you wave harder and scream louder until you realize that all the waving in the world will not make him see you. To him, you're conveniently invisible.

It doesn't matter that you practiced piano with him prior to the recital, played catch with him in the yard before the big game, or helped him to glue the final pipe cleaners to his spaceship, because now, at the culminating event, nobody is waving back. When you finally figure this out, you casually pull your hand down to your head as if all this arm waving were really just an elaborate attempt to naturally smooth down your hair. Yawning as if bored by all of the excitement, you look around nonchalantly to see if anyone noticed that your heart was just broken by a child twenty-eight years your junior.

To add salt to your festering wound, when the event is over your stepchild runs excitedly up to his bio-mom and dad, showering them with hugs and high fives, and completely ignores you.

You walk away emotionally drained. Not only has your stepchild rejected you like an unpopular playmate, but he has done so in front of his mother and the parents you are just getting to know.

The quandary that the unrequited wave leaves you in is this: If you don't wave, you look like you're not supportive; if you do wave and you're ignored, you feel like a complete dork.

Sassy Stepmother Straight Scoop

There are few experiences more depressing than being ignored by your stepchildren in public. In fact most of the stepmothers I know say that they'd rather suffer Chinese water torture at the hands of their stepkids than go through the humiliation of being completely ignored by them.

Here's the deal—the raw deal. In those instances where the biological mother is present, you will always be the outcast, the thorn in your stepchildren's side. They remember the days when their parents shared Christmas, birthdays, and baseball games together. Deep in their hearts they want to push the rewind button and go back to the way it was when their parents were married and you were off being sassy and single. Yes, they love you, but no matter how fabulous and fun you are, they need to be loyal to their own parents. So remember, while your stepchildren's allegiance to their bio-mom may feel like rejection to you, it's not—in fact it has little to do with you. The sooner you understand that, the better you will feel.

Now, about waving to the air, you'll need to keep it up for a while before anyone waves back. Eventually your stepkids will get the picture and realize that it's easier to wave to the enthusiastic woman in the stands than to ignore her. But in the meantime you'll need to take care of yourself because all of that rejection can do a number on you. I found that inviting friends along to these events really helped me to get through them unscathed. My friend Kerrie was a huge help to me in the early part of my marriage. She came with me to soccer games, birthday parties, and school functions. She was my security blanket—no matter how much the kids rejected me, she was there as my true friend.

In defense of the nonwaver, keep in mind that balancing two divorced biological parents can be tough for a child of any age. Add one or two more parents to the mix and your stepchild has a veritable waving conundrum on his hands. As harsh as it may seem, you must be an adult in these situations. The expectation that your stepchild will attend to your emotional needs is simply not realistic, particularly in the beginning. Don't rush it or push it. Your stepchild will wave back to you when he or she is good and ready.

Who Invited Her?

Connie is a stepmother who married a man who is eleven years her senior. As a result she has older stepchildren. "We met when I was thirty-four, and Kevin's daughters were twenty and twenty-two. They didn't like me from the get-go and made sure I knew it. I tried hard to endear myself to them. It just seemed the more effort I put into the relationship, the more difficult and rude they were to me. If we went to dinner, they would completely ignore me or pretend that I wasn't there. It was so hurtful. The most devastating event was when I went with my husband to one of my daughters' dance competitions and after the event she asked right in front of me, 'Who invited her?'"

Up until now I have been talking mostly about infants, preteens, and teenage stepchildren who live at least part-time with their father and stepmother. But what happens when older children who don't live with you, and who should know better, intentionally hurt you or ignore you?

Many of the stepmothers I have met over the years who marry into a family with teenagers and college age children find bonding with the kids to be especially difficult if not impossible. These stepkids have lived most of their lives with their parents and are often dumbfounded when their ostensibly normal lives are suddenly interrupted by divorce or remarriage.

Bad manners from adult children are absolutely inexcusable in my book, and the only people you have to blame for this behavior are your stepchild, your husband, and his ex-wife. So besides finding someone to blame, how do you deal with such inappropriate and hurtful behavior? First and foremost your husband is responsible for making sure you are not abused or mistreated by his kids. Ask him to sit down with them and discuss why they feel inclined to treat you badly. Make sure he tells them how hurtful their actions are to both of you.

I have a friend whose husband told his college age son that he was not welcome home to visit unless he started to treat his stepmother better. At first his son stayed away, but eventually he came back home and began treating his stepmother with respect. It's hard for divorced fathers to stand up to their kids, particularly if they feel guilty for the divorce. But if your husband does not stick up for you, you may have to set some boundaries for yourself. I know one stepmother who, after many disappointing and hurtful events with her stepchildren, put her foot down and refused to attend events with them in the future. Now when her husband sees his kids he does so without her. "It's not ideal," she says, "but I am not mistreated and my husband understands where I stand on the issue."

Sassy Stepmother Straight Scoop

Can you sing *"Don't turn around now, 'cause you're not welcome anymore . . ."*? You know the song—Gloria Gaynor's "I Will Survive" from the seventies. Well, I couldn't say it better. If you have older stepkids who egregiously mistreat you, DO NOT stick around for the abuse. Simply put your foot down like you would with any illmannered and hurtful individual and refuse to enlighten them with your presence. It's not easy and it may be hurtful for your relationship with your husband, but at least everyone will respect you for not being a big pushover. Stand your ground, and eventually either they'll learn to mind their manners and treat you with respect or they'll be forced to keep their distance.

CHAPTER FOUR

The Ex-Wife, Till Death Do You Part

Nothing ignites a conversational explosion among stepmothers more than the hyphenated six-letter word—*ex-wife*. While many of us dive into our marriages with little thought given to the woman who once shared our husband's toothbrush, we eventually discover that she's more than an interested bystander. In truth she is the *trois* in your very own ménage à trois.

Most of my single-girl-turned-stepmother friends were far more angst-ridden about whether or not they could pull off wearing a virginal white dress on their wedding day than how they would live alongside their husband's ex-wife. My prenuptial concerns, no less trivial, were centered on transportation. With two growing boys would I eventually be forced to drive a minivan? And if so, what impact would such a vehicle have on my self-image?

It didn't occur to me until much later that living within five miles of my husband's ex-wife would be far more threatening to my identity than driving a Dodge Caravan.

That said, I am here to state for the record that you can and should learn to get along with the woman who gave birth to your husband's kids. Nine out of ten stepmothers I interviewed report that the key to stepmother success is to grow up, shake off your petty inclinations toward the ex-wife, and find it within yourself to be a good sport and get along.

Hard to fathom, I know. In fact I can hear many of you choking on your diet soda at the very idea of having even the most remote regard for your husband's painfully thorny ex. Some of you may be so repulsed by the idea that you will be tempted to throw this book across the room at the very suggestion of it. If you are so inclined, go ahead—hurl it over the furniture to the far end of the room and let it land with a *thwack*. Once it hits the ground, take a breath, go pick it up, and continue reading.

Before I get to the part about how you get along with the ex-wife, let me first tell you that there was a time when the idea of being relaxed and friendly around "her" was as foreign to me as wearing white pumps in winter. Over the years, however, things have changed. More explicitly, I have changed. Rest assured, my road to enlightenment was no fast-track graduate program. In truth, it was extremely remedial, often painful, yet very revealing. Let's just say that having trudged through the muck of divorce and stepmotherhood, I have come to know myself a whole lot better.

The following are a few rules we stepmothers pulled

together to help you weather the rocky path of "ex-wife enlightenment" more gracefully than we did. Remember that it's hard to be perfect right out of the gate. Cut yourself some slack and be prepared to slip up now and then. If you find yourself fantasizing about malicious revenge that includes slander and defamation of character, remember, everything you're feeling is normal!

Rule #1: Don't Believe Everything You Hear

It is rare to find a divorced man who speaks glowingly of his ex-wife, particularly if he is a novice divorcé and part-time single dad. And it is natural for you, his soul mate, to hang on his every word as he recounts the injustices he suffered at her hands. Certainly he wouldn't be divulging such intimate stories if they weren't true—e.g., her nasty affair, her frigid character, her incessant need to floss her teeth in bed. "Poor guy," you say as you nuzzle up to him like a loyal puppy. "I'm sorry you had to put up with that. You deserve so much better."

While your man may be grateful for your empathetic ear as he weaves his tales of marital destruction, it is not likely that he intends for you to harbor the same grudge toward his ex-wife that he does. But it's hard to know exactly what he needs when he's verbally dragging over the coals the woman he once whispered sweet nothings to. Your instincts will tell you to cheer him on. "I can't believe the two of you were ever together! She sounds like a total wacko." You fuel his fire because you know that

69

anger breeds contempt, and contempt for her means only one thing for you—no shared holiday celebrations. In fact, once you get on his bandwagon of disdain, the more secure you feel in your relationship, albeit temporary.

Mary's new husband, Jon, was financially and emotionally devastated when he and his former wife split up. While he was relieved to be out of his unhealthy marriage, he was bitter and angry that he lost primary custody of his kids. Furthermore his hard-earned salary was funding her new life, and the house he had so painstakingly remodeled himself was now in her name. In the early days of their courtship Mary listened intently as the man she loved dissected his failed marriage and recounted painful stories about his ex. The more he complained about his evil ex, the more secure Mary felt in the relationship. "If the ex made him this unhappy," she told herself, "certainly he will have absolutely no regrets when he marries me."

As far as Mary was concerned, the ex-wife was a bad person on a par with the puppy-murdering Cruella De Vill. Any enemy of her flawless man was surely an archenemy of hers. Caught up in her self-serving disdain for her fiancé's ex-wife, Mary failed to see that the ex's only crime at the time was finding and marrying Jon before she did.

Over time, Jon's wounds healed, which confused Mary. He stopped feeling sorry for himself, abandoned his disdain for his ex-wife, and started to work hard on establishing a cooperative relationship with her that included, among other things, thoughtful phone conversations and quarterly coffee meetings at the local Starbucks. Ostensibly, their discussions were about logistics, but Mary couldn't accept the fact that it took thirty minutes on the phone to decide when and where the kids should be dropped off. After a few eavesdropping sessions, Mary pushed Jon to shorten his chats with the ex and stick to business.

"Hey, wait a second here. I thought you hated her," Mary reminded Jon following a successful planning session with the ex-wife.

"Oh, come on, honey, quit being so dramatic. I never said that I hated her."

To Mary, Jon's high-and-mighty "Kum-Ba-Ya" attitude was like freshly manicured acrylic nails scratching on a blackboard. His about-face change in attitude left her wondering if he had suddenly contracted a severe case of Alzheimer's disease or at the very least amnesia.

"At the time I would have been much happier had their chat sessions ended with a four-or five-letter word and an enraged hang-up rather than the affable good-byes they shared," admits Mary.

Sassy Stepmother Straight Scoop

If your husband and his ex are committed to creating a harmonious life for their kids, they will eventually set aside their hostility toward one another and start to communicate and cooperate. Be forewarned that when your man begins to play nice with his ex-wife, you may feel like your handsome and faultless Romeo has forsaken you. Desperate to reaffirm your status as priority number one, you may find yourself reminding him of all the nasty things he said about his ex-wife early on in your relationship. When you do, however, chances are he'll take the fifth and you will be left feeling like an insecure soap opera diva.

In the early stages of your courtship and marriage it will be hard for you to imagine that your ideal man had anything to do with his failed first marriage. Keep in mind it takes two to have a fight and no one comes out of a bad relationship completely fault free. That said, be sure to listen empathetically when your man digs up the dirt on his ex-wife, but try to reserve your judgment until you get a chance to know her yourself. When your husband begins to cooperate with his ex-wife, do not be threatened by their consideration of one another.

Rule #2: The Bio-Mom's Mothering Style Has Nothing to Do with You

Having never mothered before, I found the typical Friday night "drop-off" routine with the boys' mother (my husband's ex) to be absolutely excruciating and intimidating. It seemed there was so much information to grasp that I would never get up to speed on the part-time mothering routine. Conversations on the door stoop usually included a play-by-play recap of the kids' week and a detailed outline of concerns and directives that pertained to their mental and physical health, complete with bowel movement analysis. My husband's ex spoke to me like I was an inexperienced babysitter (which wasn't far off the mark) who would never grasp the nuances of child rearing.

Not entirely sure what the proper response was to the warning of "runny poop," I found myself nodding like a bobble-headed doll every time she began to impart last-minute instructions. "OK, then, uh-huh, all right, sure, OK," I responded with the deference of an undocumented foreigner not entirely familiar with the language but damn glad to have a job. I was hopeful that my enthusiastic nod and phony smile would make up for the fact that I didn't know what the hell she was talking about. She must have begun to recognize my glazed look because often the drop-offs were followed up by reminder phone calls and e-mails that reinforced her doorstep instructions.

It was an odd thing. In the ex's presence I transformed from a strong and opinionated person to the incredible shrinking woman. Bottom line, her experience as a bio-mom intimidated me to the point that I questioned everything I did and said when she was around. After all, she seemed to be the authority on mysterious kid things like allergies, soccer brackets, and whooping cough. Once when she reported that one of the boys had gotten the croup, I smiled with delight, asking, "Where did you get it done?" Little did I know, the croup was an illness and not a hairstyle. But as soon as she was out of sight my lack of experience in bio-mothering no longer mattered and I was able to welcome the children with open arms.

After about six months of daunting Friday night drop-offs, I decided I would improve my mothering skill set by boning up on all things "kiddish." I was a quick study and in no time I could spot an oncoming cold virus like an Italian handbag in a sea of domestic knockoffs. I could differentiate an authentic cry for help from a fake one in one second flat and I could whip up a healthy batch of waffles in a mere ten minutes. As far as I was concerned, I was well on my way to mastering the skills of coparenting. And yet the phone calls, wearisome child-rearing homilies, and e-mails kept on coming.

Don't misunderstand me; my husband's ex was never evil or overtly malicious. No, she was more underhanded than that, which really pissed me off. To an outsider, her need to be in touch at all times seemed harmless and benign, the qualities of a good mother. But I saw her Orwellian "Big Mother" shtick for what it was: a well-constructed strategy to keep me permanently off-balance and paranoid.

Sassy Stepmother Straight Scoop

Of course your husband's ex-wife is going to question your mothering skills. Why shouldn't she? She's dropping off her kids with you—someone she hardly knows—for an extended amount of time. In situations where you feel your mothering aptitude is being questioned, when you say things like "How dare she!" take some time to see the forest through the trees. When you do, chances are you will discover that the ex-wife is not out to ruin your good standing but to protect the well-being of her little darlings. Remember, a protective ex-wife is certainly better than someone who could not care less about the welfare of her children.

Lastly, remember that it's just not practical or flattering to carry a bitter albatross around your neck. Any aesthetician worth her salt scrub will tell you that anger creates fine lines and crow's-feet. So when you encounter the ex-wife, do something good for yourself and opt for a pretty smile rather than a furrowed brow.

Rule #3: Set Limits and Boundaries with Your Husband's Ex-Wife

In my first year of marriage, I was horror-struck by the number of times I was required to interact with the kids' bio-mom. Since I had lived in sin with my husband prior to our marriage, the ex-wife was no stranger to my world. Once our union was official, however, I assumed she would miraculously slip into the background and let me try my hand at stepmothering. Not so. Every time I answered the phone, she was there like an ex-girlfriend we couldn't shake. I found myself looking for the divorce decree in the file cabinet to make sure that it had actually happened.

With my husband's ex-wife in my periphery at all times, my newlywed year was spent in frustration. She had a maddening habit of showing up at the wrong times (my birthday) and ruining my well-constructed fantasy of being an adoring and adored newlywed. I was grumpy all the time, wearing my irritation like an ill-fitting thread-thin thong. Furthermore, I found my prince in his not-so-shiny armor to be evasive at best and spineless at worst when it came to setting some reasonable boundaries. That was until . . . a big boundary was crossed.

It was late on a workday afternoon in our second year of marriage. I had made a stop at the grocery store on my way home from work to get some chicken and broccoli for dinner. The boys were coming to stay with us and they love chicken and broccoli, especially when followed by ice cream and hot fudge.

When I pulled into our driveway I could see that there were several grocery bags on the porch. "Ahh, a gift from the neighbor," I assumed. But on closer inspection I saw that there were four bags of organic, wheatless, dairyless groceries on our porch. At first I thought it was a mistake. The people next door must have fallen for the dot-com grocery delivery that was being touted as the Second Coming. But as I struggled to work my way around the bags blocking our door, my own earth-damning groceries in tow, I recalled a conversation I had had with Mark a few days earlier. He mentioned in passing that he'd had a discussion with his ex, something about acceptable food choices for her potentially allergy-prone child.

Suddenly the mystery of the grocery fairy clicked and my wimpy niceties turned to spewing fireballs. Luckily for the both of us, the ex had already come and gone. I am certain that had she still been there, I would have thrown the organic tomatoes at her car.

I was furious as I unpacked the tofu-coated, wheatless pretzels, the boxes of soy-infused rice milk, and the cheese-free cheese. A person could say a lot of bad things about me, but no one could criticize my eating habits. I am known among friends and family for my healthy lifestyle, daily yoga routine, and abhorrence of all things McDonald's. I make it a point to eat all foods in moderation. The very suggestion that I might have neglected the needs of the children through improper nutrition was blasphemous.

When my husband got home I went ballistic and demanded in no uncertain terms that he "get her on the phone right now and tell her that she has very bad manners, and she is never allowed to do our grocery shopping for us again." I stood over his shoulder as he told her on the phone in a calm and reasonable manner that her ostensible act of kindness was not appreciated and that any future grocery delivery was out of the question.

When he got off the phone I asked, "OK, what'd she say?"

"She's worried about Gavin. There is the possibility he may have some wheat allergy."

"Well, we can buy him that stuff," I fumed. "She's just trying to make us look bad."

"Sally, she felt terrible that you were mad, and I don't really think it had anything to do with our parenting skills. I told her that while we appreciated it, her gesture was inappropriate."

"Puhleease," my Evil Twin responded, totally annoyed that he was defending her. "You told her we appreciated her gesture? You liar! I didn't appreciate it one single bit," I said, stomping away from him down the hallway. "I hope you told her that I'd personally throw the groceries out on the street if she ever tried that again," I yelled over my shoulder. "What does she think? We're too stupid to buy the right groceries?"

I was as mad as a hatter for about two weeks. I avoided all things ex-ish, including drop-offs, sporting events, and school functions. When a new-spouse–old-spouse interaction could not be avoided, my conversations with the ex were chilly and brief.

Thanks to my husband, I never actually confronted the ex-wife about the unspeakable grocery infraction, probably a good thing since I know I would have created a shameless scene that would have me cringing for the rest of my life. So instead of a nasty catfight, I opted for fantasy revenge, which in my imagination included a condescending lecture from me to the ex-wife on her deplorable manners (where I come from, telling a girl she has bad manners is akin to telling her she has suffocating body odor). While I was giving her telepathic lessons on proper social behavior, my husband, Mark, was saddled with the dirty work of sitting down face-to-face with his ex-wife at the local Starbucks to set reasonable limits and boundaries for our family.

Sassy Stepmother Straight Scoop

"Setting boundaries"—the words sound so New Age, self-helpish. Though I had heard of "having your boundaries crossed" long before Grocerygate 2000, I didn't know exactly what it meant—I just passed it off as psychobabble. Now post-Grocerygate, I understand exactly what the words mean and can sense a boundary crossing long before it happens.

My advice to you, the fledgling stepmother, is to sit down with your husband and decide what your boundaries are for your family long before your husband's ex-wife is doing your grocery shopping. Remember, she can't read minds nor can you, so all of you need to be upfront about how much interaction and "togetherness" you will and will not tolerate and what your specific rules for engagement are. My husband found that meeting with his ex-wife over coffee and calmly discussing our individual families' needs usually had a positive effect.

Finally, I know I've said this before, but you need to keep in mind that conflicts or misunderstandings with the ex-wife are rarely about you. Hard to believe when you've come from an "all about me" lifestyle. I have to admit, looking back, that I am a bit embarrassed that I thought the ex's allergy concerns were all about me. Over time I have come to see that the ex's penchant for being in my face was more likely a result of her own maternal needs than a comment on my skills as a part-time mother.

Rule #4: What Kind of Ex Would You Be?

When you find yourself ranting about something the ex-wife did or when you're just plain sick of having a third person in your relationship, ask yourself this simple question: What kind of ex-wife would I be? Whew, I shudder to think.

My friend Kristine is a summer stepmom; in other words, her teenage stepdaughter, Olivia, lives two thousand miles away with her mother throughout the year and lives with her dad and Kristine for only two months during the summer. Kristine, a successful and busy lawyer, loves the arrangement. Having never had a child of her own, she sees it as a great bonus to get some of her maternal instincts met without having to mother year-round.

One June early in Kristine's marriage, when Olivia came for summer vacation, she asked her stepmother if she could have a picture of her to take home. Kristine was delighted that Olivia wanted a personal memento. Days later, after sorting through various photos and choosing one that was particularly fetching, Kristine presented Olivia with a framed picture of herself where she appeared thin, tanned, and rested. Olivia took the picture, barely looking at the image in the frame, and dutifully tucked it in her suitcase. Surprised at her emotionless response, Kristine asked Olivia, "Honey, where do you think you'll put that picture when you get home?"

"Ummm, I dunno," Olivia stammered, her ears reddening with embarrassment.

"Don't you like that picture?" Kristine asked, confused.

"Well, it's not really for me. It's for my mom."

"Your mom wants a picture of me?"

"Yeah, since she's never even met you, she wants to see what you look like. She also wants me to find out if you celebrate Christmas. She says you have a weird last name, so you might not."

Kristine was absolutely dumbfounded. She couldn't believe that Olivia's bio-mom would go to such lengths as to send her daughter on a covert spy mission to inspect her new stepmother's appearance and investigate her religious background. "How dare she?" she asked me. I howled with laughter.

I had to laugh that Kristine, my cattiest of friends, was shocked that her husband's ex-wife would encourage such clandestine behavior. I know that if Kristine had been on the other end of this story, sending her daughter off for the summer to a woman she had never met, she would have been guilty of spying and a whole lot more.

Sassy Stepmother Straight Scoop

Imagine putting your baby on an airplane and sending her off to your ex-husband's house, where a woman you've never met is charged with her care. I quiver at the thought of leaving my cat with a stranger for a mere weekend—I can only imagine what would happen if I had to hand off my own genetic reproduction. I am sure that if I was forced to do so, however, I would be guilty of more than an amateur investigation of my ex-husband's new wife. (Can you say FBI background check? Wiretap? Hidden camera?)

When your husband's ex-wife makes you hiss like a feral cat, try to take a deep breath, close your eyes, and put yourself in her jeans for a moment. I know—it sounds easier than it is, but if you can do it, you will ultimately save yourself some anxiety. Chances are she is a woman like you, who wants nothing more in the world than to be happy, loved, and connected to her kids.

Rule #5: Never Say Never

Believe it or not, I have met many stepmothers who have become friendly with their husband's ex-wife. Some have even stayed connected long after the husband they shared is out of the picture (i.e., death or, dare I say, divorce). While I'm not sure I will ever claim good-friend status with my husband's ex-wife, I do know that the longer I am married to my husband, the closer I am to his children and the more comfortable I feel around their mother. Will my husband and I go dancing with the ex and her new husband when we're old and gray? I'm not sure. All I can say is, never say never.

My friend Nancy, much to her husband Gary's dismay, did not attend her stepson Michael's graduation from kindergarten, grade school, high school, or college. Even though her husband had made peace with Joan, his first wife, Nancy held on to her early conviction that Joan, a woman who had committed adultery and broken up a family, was despicable and not to be trusted.

Nancy thought that by steering clear of all important family events, she could avoid uncomfortable and potentially heated interactions with the deplorable ex-wife. But what she failed to realize is that by not going to the graduations, she missed out on celebrating some of life's watershed moments with her husband and stepson, Michael.

Last spring Nancy was put into an untenable position when Michael and his fiancée, Carly, announced their engagement. Nancy was ecstatic with the news; she loved Carly and was delighted at the prospect of having another woman in the family. Her elation was soon deflated, however, when Michael unfolded a dubious plan.

"Nancy, I really want you to take part in my wedding," he said with the utmost sincerity. "You have meant so much to me over the years. I would be honored to have you walk down the aisle with my mother during the wedding ceremony."

At first Nancy thought Michael, a certified prankster, was pulling her leg. The very thought of being in the same general vicinity with Joan gave Nancy enough anxiety to fuel a Woody Allen movie. Taken aback by the ridiculousness of Michael's request, Nancy looked to her husband for empathy but found that he, along with the newly engaged couple, was holding his breath in anticipation of her response. Mortified, Nancy stood to collect the empty plates, sidestepping the question with her trademark, "We'll see, honey."

Many days and weeks later, after pressure from her

son's fiancée and her husband, Nancy reluctantly agreed to the otherwise unthinkable plan. But when the day of the wedding finally arrived, Nancy's insides were in knots.

When Nancy and Gary arrived at the church, she was a wreck. Across the parking lot Nancy spotted Joan as she and her companion of ten years uncoiled themselves from their little sports car and walked hurriedly into the building.

The first person Nancy encountered when she entered the church was Carly's mother, dressed in a smart blue-and-white mother-of-the-bride number. She embraced Nancy and whispered in her ear, "We are so happy to have you be part of our wedding." As Nancy hugged Carly's mother, she saw Joan standing in front of her with a look of anticipation. When Carly's mother pulled away, Nancy was face-to-face with her lifelong nemesis Joan, who was holding out her hand and smiling like Mother Teresa.

"Thank you so much for agreeing to do this," Joan said. "I know it's probably not entirely comfortable for you, but it is really important for the kids. It was Michael's wish, and mine, too, to show you how much you mean to this family."

"It was a turning point in my life," Nancy told me. "I finally realized that I had been harboring anger for most of my adult life toward someone I didn't even know. What a relief to finally let it go."

Nancy ended up having a great time at the wedding, and the walk down the aisle with Joan was surprisingly emotional. At the reception they had a ball together, sharing stories about Michael with his new in-laws. While they are not best friends, Nancy and Joan do enjoy seeing each other every few months at various family events. Nancy's only regret is that she wasted twenty years being mad at a woman she barely knew, and missed out on getting to know one of the most important people in her stepson's life.

Many of the stepmothers I have spoken to over the years report that their husband's ex-wife "isn't that bad." Most of them have grown to appreciate and value her presence in their lives. "It takes time," says Whitney, a stepmother who once hated her husband's ex but has since learned to appreciate her. "I needed to be secure in my relationship with my husband and his kids before I was able to share the love. Once I felt that I was on solid footing in my family, I was able to see my husband's ex-wife for who she really was: a decent mother of two kids, trying to make it in the world."

Sassy Stepmother Straight Scoop

While nothing prepares you for the role of a successful stepmother, there are plenty of messages in the media and in fairy tales that will tutor you in the skills of becoming a bitter enemy to the ex-wife. As far as the Brothers Grimm were concerned, putting an ex-wife and a stepmother in the same room together was a recipe for disaster. No two women married to the same man (at different times) could possibly be civil to one another. But believe it or not, your husband's ex-wife probably has some endearing qualities—after all, he did marry her. And remember, an apple doesn't fall too far from the tree. In other words, if you like your stepchildren, there is probably something you would like about their mother, too, if given the chance.

Rule #6: Happy Wife, Happy Ex-Wife, Happy Life

When my husband makes me mad I like to remind him of the old proverb I mentioned earlier: "Happy wife, happy life." While this statement is very true in our household, it gets even more complicated for him, poor guy. His spin on the adage goes something like this: Happy wife, happy ex-wife, happy life—it's a trickle-down effect, exactly in that order.

If you're a new stepmother, try to encourage your husband to be kind to his ex. Mwa-ha-ha-ha-ha-ha, you laugh. Pure sacrilege? Not at all. I'm not implying that your husband put his wife before you. In fact, that is a certain recipe for divorce. What I am saying, however, is it is in your best interest that your husband be somewhat kind or at the very least cordial to his ex-wife.

Allow me to make my point more clearly. Close your eyes, and imagine for a moment a life with an awful witch of an ex-wife. (You may not have to imagine; you may already have one. More on that later.) Your husband is under constant stress because her wrath scares the hell out of him. Your stepkids, bless their little hearts, are freaked-out because any show of affection to you is clearly a violation of loyalty to their mother. And the joint checking account you so unwillingly decided to open with your husband is as dry as a desert due to unplanned expenses that the ex-wife sprang on your husband at the last minute. Nirvana? I don't think so.

My grandmother always used to say to me after one of her syrupy conversations with her grumpy neighbor, "You catch a lot more bees with honey than with vinegar." Same thing here. You're better off trying to make nice with the ex-wife, or simply encouraging your husband to do so, than building a moat of anger and resentment around your family. This doesn't mean that you invite her to trounce all over you in expensive footwear or find ways to take advantage of you. But what it does mean is that you encourage friendly dialogue and show her respect.

Rule #7: Happy and Hitched

This may sound like a gross generalization and an old-fashioned one, too, but most sassy stepmothers agree that the number one way to turn an unhappy ex-wife into a happy one is to get her married to a great guy or hooked up with a great woman (whatever her preference). I cannot tell you how many stepmothers I've talked to who have told me that their husbands' ex-wives became different people when they finally landed in a good relationship. "It was a magical transformation," says Candy, a stepmother from Oregon. "Once my husband's ex-wife was in a good relationship, she was off our backs. She started to actually be nice to me."

Don't be mistaken. This is not an invitation to start

pimping your husband's ex-wife or to start moonlighting as a matchmaker—I would never encourage such intimacy with the ex. What I am recommending, however, is that you be flexible on schedules as your husband's ex-wife begins to develop her personal life outside her immediate family.

I have a friend, Lynn, who gets so annoyed when she sees her husband's ex-wife: "She always shows up in the most incredible clothes—it's killing me. I just have to wonder if that's my money that's buying her Dolce & Gabbana jeans."

I say, who cares whose money is buying her too-tight jeans or her sassy sling-backs? As long as she's not egregiously overspending or neglecting the kids, let her primp and fuss all she wants. Remember, the best thing that can happen to you and to her is that she finds herself a happy, healthy relationship, one that gives her less time to stew about you.

When my friend Bridget got married, her husband's ex-wife was as mean as Medusa. Her stepson, Jack, wore the scars of a boy who had to keep his relationship with his stepmother absolutely top secret. His mother could not bear the mention of Bridget's name or even the acknowledgment of her existence (even though she was the one who wanted out of the marriage with Bridget's husband in the first place). The very thought of a personal encounter with Jack's mother made Bridget shake in her boots like a kid who knows she did something wrong but is not sure what. So instead of trying to kill her with kindness, Bridget slipped into the background like a hidden fugitive on days when Jack was picked up or dropped off.

Two years into the marriage, Jack began to mention

"Mom's boyfriend, Tom." It was Tom this and Tom that. As far as Bridget and her husband knew, Tom was some cool rock star that suddenly appeared in Jack's life. Little did they know, Tom was a five foot seven guy with an electric guitar, a gut, and a wicked sense of humor. Jack started to seem lighter and was less conflicted about going between the two houses. He clearly enjoyed his time with his mom more than he had when it was just the two of them. With his mom's boyfriend, Tom, in the picture, he was no longer her sole companion, and he could relax a bit.

One weekend shortly after Tom moved in with Jack and his mom, Bridget was helping Jack with his Spanish homework at the kitchen bar. Out of the blue, between *hojla* and *gracias*, Jack said to Bridget, "My mom wanted me to tell you hi and thank you for helping me with my homework." Bridget, dumbfounded and not quite convinced she had heard him correctly, nearly fell off her barstool. Jack, oblivious, went back to his Spanish while she took a minute to recover. When Bridget had regained her composure, she lightly pinched Jack on the arm and said, "Hey, tell your mom I think she does a pretty good job with you, too."

Since that time, Bridget has attended several events where the ex-wife is present. And the ex is always there, arm in arm with Tom, with a smile and a kind word for her. "It seems kind of ridiculous that a husband is what it took for the ex to be nice to me," she says. "But I guess it would be pretty annoying to be struggling as a single mom while your ex-husband basks openly in the glow of new love."

Sassy Stepmother Straight Scoop

Here's the deal. You want your ex-wife happy. Whether that means giving her more time in her schedule to date, creating a flexible calendar with the kids so she can go back to school, or stepping in when she wants to go on a two-week vacation. Barring any egregious requests (e.g., fixing broken appliances or shelling out dough for unplanned expenses), you and your husband should be open to accommodating her needs and in turn she will likely do the same for you. Remember, Happy ex-wife, happy life, and that goes for you, too.

CHAPTER FIVE

Who Is That Girl Anyway?

In my travels and e mail correspondence with stepmothers across America, I have been privy to both harrowing and heartwarming ex-wife stories. I can't tell you how many times I have heard, "You will never believe what my husband's ex-wife did. . . ." While some outrageous accounts do in fact make my hair curl, they fail to shock or surprise me anymore. You see, mean-spirited ex-wives are pretty much the same from state to state. The same is true for kind and well-intentioned ones. While we all like to think our situation is "the worst," or the most "unique," there are women who live five thousand miles apart with shockingly similar ex-wife stories.

The Ex-Wife Type

After hundreds of hours of dishing up ex tales with stepmothers across the nation, I saw five distinct ex-wife archetypes or personalities that consistently surfaced from story to story. The following is an outline of who's who out there in the world of ex-wives. If you read closely, I am sure you will uncover a personality type that describes your husband's ex-wife to a tee. So if you're planning on making this marriage an "until death do you part" arrangement, I suggest that you read on for insights into the personality traits of the woman you're about to spend the rest of your life with.

POOR ME! (POOR YOU!)

This is the woman who just can't let go. It seems she hasn't yet accepted the fact that she is divorced from your husband. As a result she treats your man like he's her man, and you like the nanny. Typically a more traditional person, she likely stayed at home with the kids when she and your husband were married. Even after years of being divorced, she still depends on your husband to fix her sink, manage her finances, and screw in a lightbulb. Out of pure guilt, your husband continues to care for her like a sibling with special needs. When you are all together, she touches his arm or flirts with him as if they are still sharing the same bed.

Spotting a "Poor Me"

Assigning Blame: Even though she may have left your husband, a "Poor Me!" is prone to say things to the kids such as "Before your father left me, we were one big happy family," placing the blame for the divorce on your husband and positioning you as the "home wrecker."

The "We" Factor: Another annoying feature of this prototype is her need to use the word "we." She continually refers to "we" when she is talking about anything that pertains to your husband: "We never really liked squash soup," or "We've never really considered ourselves political." Her identity is wrapped up in her old marriage and she has no concept of herself as an individual.

All in the Family: A "Poor Me" is likely to be intertwined in your husband's life at every turn, including the lives of his family, e.g., parents and siblings. My friend Lynn, who is married to Dan, who has a "Poor Me" ex-wife, finds it absolutely infuriating when she goes to her in-laws' house for dinner. "His mother talks about the ex as if she were her very own daughter, with no sensitivity to me. And to make matters worse, there are pictures of her in their foyer showing her sitting next to Dan while she's nursing their first son."

How to Handle a "Poor Me"

A "Poor Me!" is difficult because she's not mean or nasty—she's just helpless. And if you're like me, you feel there is nothing more repugnant than a woman who can't take care of herself. Three words of wisdom on this one— *get her married.* Because her identity is tied up in being a couple, the "Poor Me" will hang on to your husband until she finds someone new. Once she does, she will be surprisingly out of the picture, and you'll once again look forward to answering your phone.

Now, if finding a man for your husband's ex is going to be so much work that it competes with your day job, you'll need to come up with a less time-consuming boundary-setting strategy. Keep in mind that while it may save you hours of perusing the personal ads or going online to

Match.com, the alternative will not be as amusing or entertaining. Setting boundaries usually requires at least one face-to-face summit between your husband and his ex-wife. (If you really want to make the point, you may consider attending the meeting yourself.)

Like all good diplomatic summits, this one should be stage-managed with the utmost care and precision. You and your husband will need to define and communicate what "comfortable boundaries" and "rules of engagement" mean for your family. Consider her needs when making your list and be prepared to empathize with her needs and to compromise on some of your less important items on the list.

PSYCHO EX-WIFE (PEW)
This is the worst ex-wife prototype. But there is good news. There are far fewer PEWs than there are ex-wives of other prototypes. For those of you who are stuck with a PEW, I send my condolences. There's not much you can do with this one, other than cross your fingers and hope for a relocation package. Look at it this way: She'll be good for your character. Her nasty actions and attitude will force you to grow up and rise above the fray.

Signs of a Psycho Ex-Wife
Forever Angry: This ex-wife prototype is happier being angry with others than being honest with herself. She will try to make your life miserable, calling at all hours of the day, making impossible demands, and bad-mouthing you and your husband to the kids.

Putting the Kids in the Middle: The PEW is so psycho she

doesn't understand the importance of keeping the kids protected from parental conflict. Instead she'll ask her kids to send messages for her, for example, "Mom wants me to tell you that I need new clothes." Or "Mom wants me to tell you that you need to send more money."

Insults, Threats, and Lawsuits: The Psycho Ex-Wife is so angry that she has no couth. She will act out in ways that you could never possibly imagine, embarrassing you, your husband, and his kids in public. She is not above using words or phrases that are crude, hurtful, and downright distasteful. And lastly, she has been known to threaten lawsuits when it comes to late child support payments, custody arrangements, and anything else she can stir up.

My friend Lisa has an ex-wife who threatened to sue her husband if he took his daughter on vacation out of state to Disneyland with Lisa and Lisa's parents. "She was on board with the vacation idea for months before we left, and then two days before we were scheduled to leave, she claimed she didn't know my parents were going. She said she was uncomfortable having her daughter go on vacation with people she didn't know. We ended up not going anywhere and having my parents fly up to our house. It wasn't much of a vacation for anyone," says Lisa. "I think she just wanted us to know she had the ultimate control."

How to Handle a PEW

Finding it within your heart to respect a Psycho Ex-Wife may be out of the question. My friend Tammy, a veteran stepmother with a PEW, advises, "If you are married to a man with a nasty ex-wife, keep your money and belongings legally separated from your husband's. Once you've done that, make friends with a good counselor or legal adviser to help you with the communication tools needed to deal with a difficult person."

Erin, another stepmother who has been married to a man and his PEW for over twelve years, imparts this suggestion: "As far as dealing with her, try not to have face-to-face interactions if you can. If it can't be avoided, and she tries to engage you in an argument or dispute, simply tell her that this is not the time or the place for such discussions. Offer that if she would like to discuss it further, you would be glad to do so in the company of a professional counselor. Always keep your cool and try to take the high road. Engaging in a conversation or discussion is not likely to do anything for you or for the long-term relationship with your stepkids."

Other words of wisdom from sassy stepmothers with PEWs:

1. Hold fast to the adage "What goes around comes around."
2. Have undying faith in your marriage.
3. Say your prayers to the big stepmother in the sky.
4. Never lose sight of the fact that her reign of evil is temporary (when the kids turn eighteen, she'll be out of your hair, and you and your husband will have your life back again).
5. Burn sage. My friend Carrie says that her husband's ex-wife just drains the entire family of energy. "She's such a crazy, mean-spirited person that whenever she leaves I feel really depressed. I just

want to wipe her vibe from our house. To save my sanity, I've devised this little ritual to cleanse the air once she leaves. It's an old American Indian tradition, originally intended to rid a place of bad juju left in the wake of an evil spirit. I'm not sure whether or not it really works, but it certainly makes me feel better when I'm done."

THE GOOD MOTHER

My husband's ex-wife is a Good Mother, so I have anointed myself as an expert on this ex-wife prototype. While she's probably the most functional ex-wife on the list, she can also be the most challenging and intimidating ex for a new step-mother. She's the Mother Teresa of motherhood, making all the other bio-moms cringe with an inferiority complex. She attends every PTA meeting, field trip, and sporting event; she makes the flyers for a neighbor's lost pet, coordinates the school fund-raiser, buys the gift for the coach, and plays the school nurse when there isn't one available. She's everywhere you occasionally want to be, which makes it difficult to carve out a place in your stepchildren's lives.

Signs of a Good Mother

A Selfless Creature: While she's doing it all, like volunteering to be the team mother, the teacher's aide, and the neighborhood watch maven, you're left shaking your head wondering how she ever finds time to take a shower, shave her legs, or catch up on *People* magazine gossip. She is so giving of her time and energy that she makes June Cleaver look like Imelda Marcos.

The All-Knowing: This mom has made it her mission

not only to put her kids first but also to make motherhood a full-time career. There is no disease, virus, or in-
fection that she's not familiar with or ready to tackle. She
knows every school board member and his/her views on the
latest Head Start program. She knows the snow closure
policies, earthquake readiness alert procedures, and who's
who at the crosswalk. There is no putting one over on this
woman. With her omnipresent style, how can you compete?

Sweet As Sugar: She's nice to you and really nice to your
husband. There's nothing worse. She falls all over herself
with gracious offers to "help you out." If you had it your
way, she'd be a little less friendly and ubiquitous so you
could have some time to gather your wits as you try to figure out your role in this whole charade called stepmotherhood. Her overfriendly manner and "one big happy
family" attitude gets downright irritating and makes you
wonder, "Did they really get a divorce or am I dreaming?"

How to Handle the Good Mother

It is not hard to live alongside a Good Mother because
she just wants everyone to "get along." In the beginning
you may find that all this togetherness cramps your style
and that her constant presence in your life is suffocating.
My advice? Get some distance. While you might feel a little "snubbish" or aloof, it is necessary that you create your
own history and relationship with your stepkids that is
separate from their mother's. If you don't, you will be
destined to feeling like an overgrown sibling.

In order to find the comfortable distance I'm talking
about, you will need to drum up your own signature qual-
ity or interest that you can introduce to your kids. Pick a

unique hobby or passion and run with it. I'm a backyard gambler of sorts. I was raised on blackjack and have always fancied myself an amateur card shark. Neither my husband nor his ex-wife are "cardies," so I decided to make it my mission to teach the kids the art of the game—and it worked. We're still playing cards, though we've expanded our repertoire beyond the blackjack table and are playing more socially acceptable games such as hearts, canasta, and speed. You'd be surprised at the kind of bonding that can happen over a simple game of cards.

COOL CUCUMBER

The cool-as-a-cucumber ex-wife wants nothing to do with you or your husband. If it weren't for the child she spawned with her ex, she would have no reason to speak to him, or to you for that matter. With her new husband and family, her life is pretty perfect as long as she keeps the blemish of divorce tucked safely away. In truth, if the Cool Cucumber had it her way, you guys would be completely out of the picture and she would have full custody of the child—no perfunctory visits required.

Signs of a Cool Cucumber

It's All Business: She's not mean; she's not nice; she's all business. She rarely looks at you and directs most of her curt phone calls and conversations to her ex-husband. She has no time for niceties or shared discussions of child rearing.

Mamma's Girl: She has primary custody of your stepchild or -children, which means you have them one-third of the time or less.

Ms. Inflexibility: She is very black-and-white with things such as money, schedules, and vacations. She is unlikely to be flexible when it comes to extended holidays, weekend swapping, or payment schedules.

Her Family Takes Precedence: She is very focused on her extended family. She requires that special arrangements be made when she has family in town or when there is a family celebration. She does not grant you and your husband the same flexibility or priority when it comes to sharing the children with your families.

Dad? What Dad? She does not give much child-rearing credit to you or your husband. She rarely elicits feedback on things such as education, summer camp, or extracurricular programs. She is the voice of the family when it comes to teachers, coaches, and parents. If you and your husband want to be included in these decisions or relationships, you will need to physically insert yourself into your child's life outside of your home.

How to Handle a Cool Cucumber

This wife is most annoying because she doesn't respect you. She's high-and-mighty and actually looks down her nose at you when she decides to look at you at all. She considers herself above your husband, which by association means that you're somewhere down there below her standards.

The only way to combat feeling like an ant in her company is to treat her like a peer. Try to look her directly in the eye when you talk to her, providing you don't have to unattractively contort your body to do so. Use your best professional voice and speak directly to her. It's helpful to repeat her name a few times for effect. "Yes, Janice, I understand that you will be here at five p.m. on Sunday." (Smile.) "I'll do my best to have her packed up and ready to go, Janice. Thanks again!" The stronger and more direct you are with her, the better. Eventually (it may take years), she'll catch on and come to terms with the fact that you and your husband are simply not going to go away.

Another strategy is getting to know her husband. My stepmother friend Lori made it a point to talk to her husband's ex-wife's new husband at soccer games. "He was a really nice man with a great sense of humor. We chatted at all the games about kids, soccer, and business. He liked me and could tell from our conversations how much I loved my stepson. Eventually his respect for me rubbed off on her, too."

IDOLIZED MOM IN ABSENTIA

The Idolized Mom is a lot like the Prodigal Son. While she has basically ditched her offspring in search of more exciting pastures, her kids continue to pine for her as if she had done absolutely nothing wrong. It's maddening for you because you're the one who picked up the pieces after she flew the coop and yet she gets all the credit for being a "real mother." It's not a bad setup for her.

She's particularly irritating, not because she's in your life so much, but because she isn't, at least not on a regular basis. That means that when she does show up, the experience is completely unpredictable and foreign. At least with a Good Mother or Psycho Ex-Wife you know what you're dealing with. With the Idolized Mom in Absentia you're left in the dark and so are your stepkids. But keep in mind, no amount of shopping, card playing, or ball throwing will save you from the instant demotion you will receive from your stepkids when she finally does manage to show up on the scene. You might as well pack your bags and get on a flight to Vegas with a few girlfriends because in her presence you'll hardly be missed.

Beth, a loyal and giving stepmother, basically raised her husband's two girls while their bio-mom traveled the world in search of herself. When the girls got to be teenagers, their mother finally decided to set down roots and moved back to their same town. Beth was shocked to find that even though their mom was absent most of their lives, the girls held their bio-mom in high esteem. When the oldest of her stepdaughters graduated from high school, there was a limited number of tickets allotted to each family—one for each parent. It broke Beth's heart when her stepdaughter designated the two tickets for her bio-mom and her father.

Paige, another stepmother who is saddled with an IMIA, basically raised her stepdaughter, Jessica. She remembers a time when she tried to cover up for her husband's ex-wife. "At first I did it because I didn't want Jessica to be sad. If her mother would forget her birthday, which she did almost every year, I would go out and buy a stuffed animal or something and sign the card 'Love, Mom.' It was totally dishonest, but it was all I could do to keep from seeing little Jess disappointed one more time. When she got a little older Jessica figured out my cover-up strategy. But rather than feeling more endeared to me for my clandestine effort, she felt duped. Not only was she annoyed with her mom's absence, but she was suddenly mad at me for being an accomplice in her mother's 'big fat lie.' While it wasn't my intention to deceive her, she felt that I had."

Being honest with your stepkids may seem a little harsh, but when they ask you over and over again why their mother didn't send them a birthday gift or show up on time on Christmas Eve, you're going to be expected to tell them something. A simple "I don't know why she doesn't send you a gift, honey" is better than making up a fabricated story that will eventually come back to haunt you and your stepchild.

Signs of an Idolized Mom in Absentia

You Are the Mother: She has given over custody of her children to her ex-husband. And as a matter of circumstance you are the one left to handle the day-to-day duties of raising her child or children.

Your Kids Are Returned Exhausted: On the rare occasion that the kids do get to spend time with her, they return worn-out and disheveled.

Her Schedule Rules: She's completely insensitive to anyone else's schedule except her own, and has been known to call or show up at a moment's notice.

Flaky: She's unreliable and changes plans at the last minute, leaving you to deal with disappointed and confused children.

Fair-weather Friends: When she shows up on the scene, your kids suddenly demote you to nothing more than Dad's wife.

Bragging Rights: Your children brag about her like she's a newly discovered rock star, which makes you feel like a has-been.

How to Handle an Idolized Mom in Absentia

The best way to deal with an Idolized Mom in Absentia is to be direct—with everybody, including your stepchildren. I'm not suggesting that you malign the ex with her kids, but I am recommending that you be truthful with them about their mother's behavior and how it impacts your family. Also, it is not out of the question for you and your husband to set down rules of engagement and expectations for her. Here are a few rules of engagement from stepmoms who have found themselves in this situation.

- All plans that include spending time with the children must be made one week in advance. This alleviates any short-term planning that might have you running around like a chicken with your head cut off. It also gives your stepchildren time to mentally prepare for seeing their mother.
- Forty-eight-hour notice on all cancellations.
- No calls after nine p.m. or before eight a.m.
- Naps and schedules must be taken into account on days that she has the kids.
- Promises are to be kept with the children. If the bio-mom cannot fulfill a promise, it is expected that she will make a phone call to the child and give him/her an explanation.

Sassy Stepmother Straight Scoop

No matter what kind of ex-wife your husband has, you can learn to manage around her and become a happy and successful stepmother. Just remember, knowledge goes a long way, and the better you understand what makes the ex tick, the more prepared you will be for unforeseen hazards down the road.

CHAPTER SIX

Finding Your Inner Disciplinarian

*M*ost stepmothers would like to think that they can effectively rule their roost without dirtying their hands with discipline. "After all," you convince yourself, "they're not my kids, so why should I be expected to reprimand them when they talk back, borrow the car without asking, or say the *f* word?" You might as well just leave the unsavory details of child rearing to the biologicals. Right? Wrong!

If you relinquish all discipline responsibilities to your husband, you may find yourself terrified by his cute little hellions and holed up like a scared prisoner in your master bedroom when he's not home. It's simply not practical or feasible to expect your paramour to drive the moral compass or protect you from inappropriate behavior at every turn, especially if you are a stepmother who spends more time with your husband's kids than your hubby does. What's more, if you bow out of discipline entirely and leave the dirty work to your man, you will be subject to his idea of appropriate behavior, which may be a bit different from your own.

There is no way around it: Disciplining children who are not your own is ambiguous, particularly when you're not terribly interested in the job, you have no child-rearing experience, and no one has officially given you the title "queen of discipline." Furthermore, most children are not looking for another parent to boss them around, so it is likely that anything you say to them regarding discipline or manners will be met with rolled eyes or comebacks like "You're not the boss of me," neither of which is a warm incentive for a woman who just wants to be liked or even loved by her husband's kids. There will be times when giving them candy at breakfast, letting them watch television way past their bedtime, or allowing them to ignore their curfew will seem like a small price to pay for their affections. But giving in to their every whim is a slippery slope. If you ever want to be taken seriously by your stepkids, you will have to learn to say no to them and to occasionally reprimand them for inappropriate or disrespectful behavior. Remember, in the absence of a biological parent, you are the boss. The sooner you get comfortable with the role, the easier life will be for both you and your family.

Establishing Your Style

When I first got married, the secondhand-parent gig seemed like a pretty good setup for me. I hung out with the boys when I felt like it and escaped with my girlfriends to the movies or dinner when responsibility loomed. I gladly left tough tasks like slapping their wrists and doing the family laundry to their father and conveniently assigned myself the role of Fun Monkey. The only fly in the ointment was that my stepkids began to think of me as an overgrown class clown rather than someone who was entitled to wield authority in her own house.

The first time my oldest stepson, Guy, rested his muddy feet on the living room ottoman, I let it slide with a tousle of his hair and a stern "Hey, you, Mr. Mud, no footwear on the furniture." He giggled. The second time, I told him, "You're walking on thin ice, kiddo. Next time I see your muddy feet on anything but the porch landing, I'll brand you like a heifer." He laughed. The third time, I decided to resort to something more serious. "If you so much as think about putting your disgusting sneakers on the furniture again, I am going to take all your Pokémon cards and give them to your brother. But before I do that, I am going to lock you in the scary, dark, cat box basement until you beg for mercy. You got it, Mr. Smarty-pants?" He looked at me curiously, not sure if he should laugh out loud or call his mom. After a second he responded with a grin. "You're not the boss of me."

I realized at that moment that my Joan Rivers, Fun Monkey routine wasn't working for anyone, especially me. And I was fearful that if I didn't get it in check, I would come home one day to find my stepsons, permanent markers in hand, transforming our hardwood floors into an NBA regulation basketball court. So in an effort to preserve both my home and my image and to thwart any neighborly calls to child protective services, I ditched my act as the household jester and became, much to my chagrin, the family shrew.

It didn't take long for me to see that being a hard-core disciplinarian wasn't really in my blood. I found myself waffling on rules to the point that even I was confused on what behavior would or wouldn't fly in my own household. Was there eating allowed in any room other than the kitchen or not? Though I had adamantly set down the hard-and-fast rule "Absolutely no consuming of any substance, be it liquid or solid, in any room other than the kitchen," I occasionally slipped and allowed the kids to eat ice cream in the TV room. At one point my eldest stepson actually asked me, "Hey, Sal, is ice cream food?" I found the more hard-core I tried to be, the less I liked myself and the less the kids respected me or understood my role.

I continued to struggle. I wanted my stepchildren to like me, but I also wanted them to take me seriously. Being a hard-ass didn't seem to work, but neither did being the class clown or the sassy best friend (I didn't even take a crack at the doting-mother act, though I have heard that many stepmothers unsuccessfully try that hat on, too). Exhausted from trying to be something I wasn't, I decided on a more novel approach—being myself. And over time (it was about three years) a consistent role developed for me. Now, instead of the Family Shrew, I fit somewhere between Authoritative Auntie and Cool Chiquita. I am also the maven of style, the mistress of manners, and the stickler for schoolwork. My days of being a simple bystander or the family killjoy are gone. Now all I need to say is "Listen, mister" and the kids know I mean business.

And business in our household means no back talk, curse words, or talking with your mouth full. Farting and burping are absolutely taboo at the dinner table, and daily niceties such as "good morning," "please," and "thank you" are mandatory. In addition, there is categorically no walking on the furniture, imaginary basketball rebounds in the kitchen, or twenty-four-hour video game-athons. We expect to know where the boys are at all times and keep a tight rein on where they can and cannot go in the neighborhood. Those are the rules in our house, and believe it or not, the kids are perfectly OK with them. And the best part is, they still seem to like me.

Sassy Stepmother Straight Scoop

Establishing a style of discipline is not easy. Most bio-moms are given the luxury of developing their parenting style over the course of their child's first few years. You, on the other hand, will have to figure it out more quickly. If you're like me and came into your marriage with little parenting experience, you may have to try on a few different disciplinarian styles before you settle on one that works for you, your husband, and his kids. But if it is any consolation, kids want boundaries, even if they're set by their stepmother. They're not apt to hate you, at least not in the long run, when you set up consistent and reasonable expectations for them. It also helps if your husband backs you up at every turn (more on that later). Remember, when it comes to discipline, conviction and consistency will rarely fail you.

The United Front

"When we all moved in together it was tough," says Julie, a stepmother of three children. "No one in my new family was terribly excited about washing their hands before dinner, doing their homework, or refilling the toilet paper on my account. It never occurred to me that it would be so difficult to command authority in my own house. As it turned out, my husband held all the cards when it came to discipline and I was basically empty-handed. It really made me mad at him. He made no effort to reinforce my role with the kids as a person with clout."

Julie's challenges are typical of women who get married without discussing discipline expectations before they tie the knot. They just assume that when everyone moves in together it will be hunky-dory. Not so. Most of the successful stepmothers I talked to agree that you can never assume things will automatically go your way. The more up-front planning and conversations you have with your husband, the more prepared you and your family will be when you come up against issues of discipline and respect.

Grace, a stepmother of two school-aged daughters, nearly flipped out when she heard her nine-year-old stepdaughter, Shelly, use the *f* word. She grimaces when she tells the story. "Normally Shelly is a sweet, well mannered child. I had never so much as heard her say 'Shut up' to her sister, let alone curse. So it really surprised me when she said the *f* word out loud. We were driving home from school, just the three of us, when I asked the girls how their day was. Shelly immediately launched into a rambling story about someone at school who got in a fight, blah, blah, blah. With one ear in the conversation and one on the radio, I kind of lost track of who was who in her long drawn-out tale. Just as I was drifting off, I heard Shelly say emphatically, 'And well, like, Johnny T——, he's a fuc——r.' 'Excuse me?' I asked. 'I said, "Johnny T——, he's a fuc——r,"' she repeated, putting extra emphasis on the *er*.

"I couldn't believe my ears. I immediately pulled over to the side of the road and read my foulmouthed step-daughter the riot act. 'We don't use that kind of language in our family! You should know better. When we get home you're going straight to your room and when your dad gets home we'll discuss how long you'll be grounded!' I was shaking—I was so mad. Shelly looked at me like a deer in the headlights. 'I'm sorry,' she said sheepishly, and then added, 'But he is.' We drove home in silence."

Later, when Grace's husband, Jeff, came home and heard the story, he was pretty upset that Grace had reacted so harshly. He told her, in no uncertain terms, that her style of discipline was not acceptable to him. And then, if that wasn't demeaning enough, he went into Shelly's room and apologized for Grace's behavior and assured Shelly that she would not be grounded. "He made me feel so terrible," recounts Grace. "Like I didn't have the first clue about parenting. But in my opinion there should be strict consequences for using the *f* word at that age."

Eventually Grace and her husband, Jeff, sought out a workshop taught in their town by a family counselor, called How to Discipline with Love and Kindness. "The workshop really helped us. We were able to discuss our expectations on neutral territory. I found out that Jeff was afraid to discipline the girls because he thought he'd lose them. And I finally revealed that I was afraid of being disrespected by his children. We also learned that we both have different styles, neither of which is right or wrong. We were able to discuss the strengths and weaknesses of our individual approaches and find a place that both of us could work from. We developed a consistent plan and some clear expectations and guidelines for us and for the kids. Now when it comes to discipline we are able to support one another rather than oppose one another."

When I asked my veteran stepmother friend Jennifer how she managed to hold down the fort with three boys, she sighed and shook her head. "It wasn't easy. My husband was at work a lot, so he and I determined that I would become the primary caretaker when they were with us. My style from the get-go was firm, which he supported. I knew that I could always dial back the strictness more easily than I could crank it up. It seemed to work so I stuck with it. The boys didn't always like me, but they respected me. Later, when they became teenagers and started challenging me more, my husband and I decided that I needed to step back and let him become the lead disciplinarian. It worked."

Sassy Stepmother Straight Scoop

It's hard to be the queen of your castle when the king, the sole omnipotent ruler, is afraid of upsetting his subjects, and your idle threats fall on deaf ears. No wonder you feel more like Joan Crawford than Carol Brady. Before there is consistency and conviction, there must be a united front. What I mean by this is you and your man need to develop a concise plan on how you are going to approach tough issues with the children. For instance, how will you reprimand them, and what are the strategies for authority? Will you be expected to set down ground rules with the kids when your husband's not around? If so, are you given full authority when he's gone? Which one of you will be the heavy when it comes to grades and chores? Will you both be responsible for demanding daily manners and niceties? How will you respond when your kids say the *f* word in your presence?

Don't forget, along with a plan, you'll need to decide on a discipline style that is acceptable to both of you. Will you be strict no-nonsense parents or will you be more relaxed and flexible? Will you impose harsh consequences for unacceptable behavior or will you use discussion and reason to reprimand? Whatever you decide, the two of you will be well served to discuss your philosophies on discipline long before you butt heads over how to handle a temper-tantrum-throwing child, a pot-smoking twelve-year-old, or a sexually active teen. Once you're good and ready to roll out your plan, sit down with your kids and share with them who exactly wears the discipline pants in the family. If you decide that your husband is going to be the key disciplinarian, make sure you get cocaptain status and that your stepkids understand exactly what that means.

"Make sure the 'Respect your stepmom' message comes in loud and clear from their dad," says Grace. Some dads feel guilty about the situation their kids are in and let their kids behave in a way that is inappropriate. It doesn't set a good example for the kids, and it could make your life miserable. You deserve respect and some authority, especially when you're in your own house!

The Innkeeper—Divvying Up Household Chores

OK, let me get this straight. You pay half the mortgage, balance the family budget, and get food on the table for your husband and his kids, yet your stepchildren don't offer to load the dishwasher, clean the sheets, or empty the laundry basket? What is wrong with this picture?

Nowadays, when anyone asks me, "What's the hardest part about raising someone else's kids?" I say, "Laundry." In our family of athletic and active boys and two busy adults we usually have at least one load of laundry going at all times. When I was single I did one load of laundry every Sunday night and that was it. Today if I left the laundry to the end of the week, I would spend an entire day and night sorting, spot removing, and folding.

In truth, on the weeks that the boys are with us, we run a virtual Laundromat out of our recreation room, which includes the never-ending pile of unfolded clean laundry on the sectional couch in front of the TV. On any given afternoon my oldest stepson can be found either next to or on top of the clean pile of clothes, clicking the remote from one baseball game to another. It makes me crazy to see him melting on the couch, oblivious to the pile made up of his baseball uniforms, jockstraps, and unmatched socks. I know that he will not fold the clothes on his own and that I will have to roust him out of his sports stupor in order to get him to match one pair of socks.

And when he finally gets motivated to move an arm toward the laundry, it's in slow motion. "Uhhh, Sally, maaaaaannnnnn, you always make me work," he says with contorted facial expressions only a preteen boy can muster. You would think I had asked him to pull a sled of coal up the side of a mountain rather than fold his baseball pants.

Now, I know mothers of teenagers across America will tell you that this is perfectly normal behavior for a preteen boy. But I am not the mother of this preteen boy. And while he is not at our house 24-7, he does have his own room, free rein in the kitchen, and a hundred percent control of the television remote. In other words, he does live with us as a family member and not a houseguest. Unfortunately, getting him to understand that concept requires a little oomph from the evil stepmother. But rest assured, when the laundry piles so high that I can barely see him covered in the underwear and socks, I have no qualms about unleashing my Evil Twin. It's not always fun, but on most days the laundry eventually gets folded.

If your stepchildren are with you only part-time, it is likely that their visits come supersized with emotional expectations for all of you. "The first year we lived together,

I literally felt like a hotel maid," says Dory, a stepmother friend with two stepsons and a stepdaughter. "But I only have myself to blame for that. I felt so much pressure to make the kids happy when they came to visit us. I wanted them to enjoy themselves at our house so they'd look forward to coming back again. The last thing I wanted to do was hound them to pick up their clothes or clean the bathroom sink. After about a year of picking dirty laundry off the floor and wiping used dental floss out of the sink, I became less interested in making my husband's kids happy and more interested in maintaining my own sanity. Finally I put my foot down and demanded that we establish some house rules and divvy up household chores. Initially the kids dragged their feet, but now they're pretty helpful and I'm sane."

Custodial stepmothers seem to have an easier time imparting discipline and assigning chores to their stepchildren simply because they live together 24-7. Establishing a routine around chores is more complicated when a stepmother has her stepchildren only part-time.

"In the beginning it was just easier to pick up after them than to try to twist their arms to help me out," says Stephanie, a stepmother who used to struggle with including her three stepchildren in day-to-day household chores. "They were only with us ten days out of the month, so creating a routine that worked for all of us was difficult, particularly when my husband and I were used to doing the chores ourselves. It was Dad and Stephanie's diner and entertainment center every other weekend. The only problem was that my husband and I were the chefs, waitstaff, cleanup crew, television referees, and Xbox monitors. It didn't take long for that to get really old.

"Eventually both of us began to dread our exhausting weekends with the kids and realized we needed to change a few things. My husband and I discussed reasonable household rules and expectations for the kids and put them down on paper. And then over dinner one night we laid down Dad and Stephanie's new 'law of the land' and then we had them sign it, like a contract. Initially the kids moaned and groaned, but they quickly caught on and began pitching in on a regular basis. Our little household-rule contract has literally changed how we function as a family. The kids understand our expectations for them around chores and discipline—no negotiations, no questions."

It all sounded so flawless, so regimented. I demanded that Stephanie give me a copy of her rules so I could show my stepsons that I wasn't the only stepmother who demanded some household rigor. Stephanie gladly printed out a copy for me at my request and now, as per her sassy stepmother approval, I'm passing it along to you.

Dad and Stephanie's Household Rules

1. Daddy and Mommy/Stephanie love all the children, no matter what the children say or do.
2. All children agree that the adults in the house (including babysitters) are in charge, and have the final say in issues, no matter what.
3. All children and adults will treat each other with respect.
4. Everyone agrees not to grab toys or other items out of other people's hands.

5. We all agree to allow others to use our own toys and to appropriately take turns.
6. Everyone agrees to always tell the truth.
7. Everyone agrees to apologize when appropriate and accept the apologies of others.
8. Food is allowed only in the kitchen and family room.
9. Everyone brushes their teeth in their upstairs bathroom.
10. Everyone puts away their own bicycle.
11. Everyone puts their own dirty laundry down the laundry chute after taking it off.
12. Everyone puts their own dirty dishes in the kitchen sink.
13. Everyone carries their trash out of cars and puts it in a trash can.
14. Everyone washes their hands with soap before touching food and after going to the bathroom.
15. Everyone will help others with reading, math, etc.
16. In this house, we say "yes" rather than "yeah."
17. No kicking a ball of any size inside the house.
18. No playing at all in the offices, except when using a CD-ROM on a PC.
19. All toys, art projects, etc. are to be put away ten minutes before leaving Dad and Stephanie's house and going to Mom's house.
20. When an adult says it's time to sleep, the decision is final—no negotiation.
21. Everyone agrees that following these rules will create a happy, healthy, and fun household.

Date: Agreed to by:

_____   _____

Dad   Stepmother

_____   _____

Child #1   Child #2

_____

Child #3

Sassy Stepmother Straight Scoop

First of all, it's your house, right? And if I'm not mistaken, you are a grown-up, correct? If you answered yes to both questions, you have my permission and the permission of mothers and fathers all over this nation to go ahead and set the rules and regulations for appropriate behavior in your household. My way or the highway? You bet.

It takes a while to feel your own power when it comes to running a household with stepchildren around. But remember, the kids are living with you at your house. Certainly, it's your stepkids' house, too, and you want them to feel welcome, but not at your expense. If you fancy yourself a domestic diva and find that your standards are much higher than your husband's, you will need to teach your family how to abide by your rules when they're in your house, e.g., wet towels are always picked up, clothes are put in the hamper, muddy shoes are left on the porch, and so on. It won't be easy and don't expect everyone to be perfect all the time, but with a little nudging, lots of consistency, and support from your husband, you're bound to arrive at a place where you can all live comfortably.

Exerting Your Influence

When I asked my friend Jan what she liked best about being a stepmother, her eyes welled with tears of pride. "I loved being able to watch my stepdaughter grow from a child into a young woman. She is a responsible, kind, and open-minded person. I know her parents had a huge effect on how she sees the world, but I know that I had something to do with it, too. It's such a great feeling to know that you've helped to shape a wonderful human being."

Face it—raising a child is a pretty big responsibility. Not only are you helping to feed and clothe the little rascals, but you're also, depending on the age of your stepkids, likely to have a big impact on how they view the world—not something to be taken lightly.

One day while we were driving home from school my youngest stepson asked me, "Sally, why are you so lucky?" It has become a bit of a joke in our family about how lucky I am. I get free parking, I win raffles, and I often clean everyone's clock when playing cards. To Gavin's question I responded, "I am lucky because I believe I am lucky. I'm also lucky because I know you guys, and you're lucky because you know me." We went round and round on the ride home pondering the possibility of thinking yourself lucky. I explained to both him and his brother my personal philosophy on luck. "Here's the deal, boys. Listen closely. If you feel lucky, you're bound to test your luck more often than the person who doesn't feel lucky, which just increases your chance of luck." Their eyes glossed over and they scratched their heads. I was certain that I had lost them on my confusing little luck lesson until later that week when I heard Guy tell his dad, "You know what? I think I'm pretty lucky. I really do." When I heard that, I had to smile. If I can help a young boy feel like he is lucky, I've done my job.

Along with the luck idea, I have also worked very hard to instill a modicum of manners in our household. I have a great book I highly recommend called *365 Days of Manners Kids Should Know.* I like to read it aloud to my stepsons at the dinner table now and then. I randomly pick a rule out of the book and read to them as if they were my attentive students in a classroom. My lessons are always met with rolling eyes and "Oh, brother—not manners again." The boys like to get my goat by egregiously talking with their mouths full or using their fingers to eat pasta. But when we are at a restaurant or at a friend's house for dinner I am proud to see that our boys are extremely well behaved. It is not uncommon for one of them to flatter the hostess with something akin to, "Jan, this chicken is so good. I think it is the best chicken I've ever had!" Often we get a phone call the following day from our hostess commenting on the boys' good manners. I like to believe that in some ways I'm partially responsible for that.

Kids are like sponges. There's no way around it. What you do, say, or show them will have an impact on their future. So it is important that you decide what sort of influence you would like to have. In our house I am the manners maven, grammar goddess, and enthusiastic show tune fan. I am always at the ready with a manners quiz, a conjugation, or a Judy Garland favorite. My hope is that one day when my stepsons are adults, they will be at an important event and someone will commend them on their impeccable manners, their elegant elocution, or their highly evolved repertoire of show tunes, and they will think to themselves, "Sally's lessons were worth it." Bottom line: As a stepmother you will have an impact on your stepchild or -children; best that you try to make that impact something you can both be proud of.

Sassy Stepmother Straight Scoop

While you may not always feel like you have any impact or influence on your stepchildren, you can rest assured that they will be watching you closely and picking up on your cues. Don't overlook the long-term effect your love, care, and moral guidance can have on their impressionable minds. That goes for your occasional unsavory behavior, too. Keep it clean, keep it kind, and keep it interesting and they'll come home one day to thank you.

Conflicting Core Values

We all come into stepmotherhood with our own set of core values that we have developed in our lifetime. Unfortunately your husband, his ex-wife, and her new mate (if she has one) may not share your same values. "My husband's ex-wife allowed my stepdaughter to go on a date when she was fourteen. I was absolutely dumbfounded. If it were up to me, she wouldn't be allowed to date until she was sixteen, and then it would be under tight supervision," says Jill, a stepmother of a precocious teenage daughter.

No matter what, there are going to be times when you disagree with how your husband and his ex-wife handle their children. And while you may pull your husband aside and tell him all the reasons why you think it's a bad idea for your stepchild to go on an overnight camping trip with a child you don't trust, ultimately he and his ex-wife must make the final decision together. "I often feel like a lobbyist," says Diana, a stepmother from Hawaii. "If I want to impact a decision that concerns the children, I pick my timing and my location carefully and then I strategically lay out my case. I know I'm a bit stricter than my husband and his ex, but I figure the combination of my 'square' perspective along with their more liberal approach usually results in a decent decision for the kids. Ultimately it works, but it's not easy.

"One night over dinner my stepson Tim, who is a senior in high school, announced that he and his buddies were planning on renting a limousine and hotel room for prom night," says Diana. "According to Tim, 'everybody's parents' were letting them do it. Aside from the fact that it was going to cost someone an arm and a leg to pick up the tab for a tux, corsage, limo, dinner, and the hotel, it just didn't seem appropriate for a seventeen-year-old boy to be alone with his friends and his girlfriend in a hotel room all night. Later that evening I sat down with my husband and calmly shared my concerns about the idea with him. Eventually he came around and agreed with me. Several days later he sat down with his ex-wife and discussed the topic with her. Apparently she was uncomfortable with the teenage plot in the first place and was somewhat relieved when we decided to be the 'bad guys.' We settled with Tim on an acceptable alternative. He could do the dinner and a limousine but had to be home that night at two a.m. He wasn't too pleased at first, but in the end he was fine with the decision."

Fran, another stepmother I know, is absolutely sick about the fact that her sixteen-year-old stepdaughter, Leanne, is already having sex with her boyfriend and that her mother supports it. "When my husband's ex-wife told us what was going on I was appalled. Just two years earlier Leanne was playing with her Barbie dolls and doing puzzles. In my opinion she was emotionally way too young to be having sex. I begged my husband to step in and do something, but he just hemmed and hawed. He said he'd rather defer to his ex-wife on the matter. I was completely distraught. Leanne and I have a fairly close relationship and I wanted her to at least understand my perspective on the issue. Several days later, when she and I were alone in the kitchen cooking, I broached the subject with her.

" 'Leanne,' I said kindly, 'I was talking to your mother last week and she told me that you and Travis were having an intimate relationship. Is that true?'

"She looked down at the cutting board and responded shyly, 'Yeah.'

" 'Travis is a nice boy. I know he wouldn't do anything to hurt you.'

" 'Fran, nothing is going to happen to me.'

" 'But I worry about you. Sex can be a very emotional thing. I wouldn't want you to get your heart broken or have something happen to you that you weren't entirely comfortable with.'

" 'My mom is OK with it.'

" 'I know she is, but having sex before you're old enough just isn't something I agree with.'

" 'Well, you're not my mom,' she said, rolling her eyes and dramatically sighing as if it was the most boring conversation in the world.

" 'Well, that's just my opinion. I hope you know you can always come to me or your dad if you have any concerns or questions.'

"She shook her head and smirked. And that was it. It wasn't the most comfortable or chatty conversation we've ever had, but I needed her to know where I was on the topic. Ultimately I think it was good for her to hear another loving adult's perspective."

Sassy Stepmother Straight Scoop

Your husband and his ex-wife are bound to make certain child-rearing decisions that will challenge your
core values. When they do, you have two options. You
can bite your tongue or offer up your unsolicited
opinion. I have learned over the years that opposing
every small decision, like whom the children are allowed to play with, often creates more problems than it
solves. Other times I have found that the decisions my
husband and his ex-wife make are too big to brush
aside, so I make my opinions known. My husband and
my stepkids don't always welcome what I have to say or
agree with me, but at least they know where I stand.

CHAPTER SEVEN

Holidays, Celebrations, and Vacations

A h, you've got to love the holidays. Christmas, Hanukkah, Halloween, and Mother's Day—revered days fraught with family friction whether you're in a stepfamily or not. Before I met my husband, the only time I lamented my singlehood was when I went Christmas shopping alone. Surrounded by festive families and couples thronging the malls, I couldn't help but feel a tad bit sad and lonely. I come from a big family, so I should have known better. Behind the shopping-induced festive facade lurked heightened sibling rivalry, in-law stress, and a high likelihood of a holiday hangover. Add a stepparent, an ex-wife, and stepchildren to an all-American family and you have a petri dish for dysfunction. That is, unless you have planned carefully for each holiday. Remember: Proper preparation prevents a surly stepmother.

I grew up surrounded by creative and resourceful teachers. My mother, my grandmother, and her eight sisters collectively logged in 260 years of teaching six-, seven-, and eight-year-olds. As a result I was trained to greet every holiday season with scissors, glitter, construction paper, and a can-do attitude. My three siblings and I showed off our talents in the front windows: snowflakes and wise men in December, pumpkins and witches in October, heart-shaped doilies and chubby cupids in February. Pity the pinched babysitter who dared enter our house on St. Patty's Day wearing anything but head-to-toe green. I learned from my grandmother and great-aunties, who sported seasonal holiday brooches on their lapels at every festive occasion, that holidays are what make the world go round. And while pagan holidays inspired fervor and zeal in our household, nothing could hold a candle to Christmas and Easter. These were major events to be seized with gusto.

Needless to say, when I married Mark and his little family I had visions of feasts at Christmastime, adulations on Mother's Day, and a red carpet on my birthday. I learned quickly that I was lucky if they remembered to leave the seat down on the toilet, let alone remember the day I was born.

It makes me cringe to think about our first Christmas together. We spent it in front of the television, Mark and his kids dressed in jeans and T-shirts, me in a festive fur-trimmed sweater and my grandmother's bejeweled Christmas brooch. We ate with plates of salmon on our laps, watching *The Return of the Jedi* and refereeing two unruly boys. Had it not been for the Christmas tree in the corner and my mistletoe earrings, it might well have been an ordinary school night instead of the world's most celebrated day.

Clearly this was not my idea of a wonderful life. I spent the latter part of the evening crying in my bedroom and longing to be back in the bosom of my own wacky family, where everyone was overdressed, overdrunk, and steaming mad at my father for his annual right-wing Christmas rant.

It took me a while to understand that my new family's laissez-faire attitude toward celebrations was not an elaborate conspiracy to ruin my good time—they had simply not inherited the holiday gene. In fact, believe it or not, their apathy had nothing to do with me. They were just going about their lives as they had been before I showed up. Since that time, however, after a lot of hard work and communication, my family and I have enjoyed many festive holiday events that would make my grandmother and great-aunties applaud from on high. Let it be known that Mark and his boys have become fervent Christmas light aficionados. Our house now emits so much Christmas cheer during the month of December, I'm afraid we may single-handedly overload the grid and send Seattle into a blackout.

How did the transformation happen? Well, it didn't happen overnight. Things didn't get better after our first Christmas together—in fact they got worse. It took a string of missed birthdays, forgotten anniversaries, and near silences on Mother's Day before I decided to take holiday matters into my own hands. I finally realized that unless I taught my family how to celebrate my way, we would be destined to do it their way. It was not that they didn't want to be festive. They just didn't know how.

There is a presumption when you marry into a family

that you will naturally blend your traditions. Not so. Remember, your family is marrying one person. You are marrying several people. It is easier for them to fold you into their customs than for them to accept yours. That's why it's so important to communicate your expectations.

My friend Nancy, a successful businesswoman and stepmother, suffers every year when her stepkids and her husband forget about her birthday and Mother's Day. She thinks her family should automatically remember her on these days without being prompted. I agree with her technically—they should remember, but they don't. My guess is she will continually be disappointed until she makes it a point to remind them of the dates and give guidelines on how to execute a terrific Mother's Day or birthday.

Sassy Stepmother Straight Scoop

If you've never been married or been a mother before, you might not realize that you have holiday expectations. Trust me, you do. It may take some time for you to recognize how you want to be treated and how you expect to treat your new family members on these precious days. But when you do, you will need to get specific and you will need to tell your clan more than once.

Don't be afraid to art direct your own birthday celebration with Martha Stewart specificity: eggs Benedict in bed, gerbera daisies and daffodils at noon, and a night complete with steak, sunset, and sultry romance.

I have learned that to have a happy holiday of any

kind I need to prepare myself and my family in advance. I start planning for Thanksgiving in October. My little monsters and I make a game of it. We plan menus, call each other "turkey" for a month, and debate the appropriate day to launch Christmas carols. Is it Thanksgiving Day or the day after?

On November 26 I start planning for Christmas, and in March I start preparing my husband and his boys for my May birthday. And the same kind of planning goes for their birthdays, Valentine's Day, and Easter. Speak up! Grab your people by the horns and let them know what you need, loud and clear. If you don't, you are guaranteed to be lost and quickly demoted from sassy stepmother to forgotten martyr.

Whose Christmas Is It This Year?

The question of who gets the kids on the holidays seems to be an overriding issue for many stepmothers. Portia, a stepmother friend who met and married a Canadian (she lives there now), has an ex-wife who rigs the holiday schedule every year so that on Christmas Eve and Christmas Day she gets the kids. Portia retells me the story for the umpteenth time: "It's always something diabolical. She uses her grandmother's health as a way to make my husband feel guilty. For the past four years she has warned that 'this time' might be Grandma's last Christmas with the kids. We get the consolation prize—Boxing Day, which might as well be called Retail Hell Day. Have you ever spent the day after Christmas with a preteen and a teenager? They invariably show up with food and family hangovers and reports that good ol' Granny is kicking up her heels on the dance floor. I come away feeling completely and totally ripped off and pissed at my husband for not standing up to the ex!"

Sassy Stepmother Straight Scoop

The advice I have for Portia and those of you out there who have a similar situation is to investigate your husband's original parenting plan. For those of you who don't know what a parenting plan is, it is a legally binding document that most divorce lawyers insist upon at the time of divorce. It explains in specific detail the rules that are required by both parties in dividing custody of the children. Most parenting plans outline the agreed-upon holiday parameters. My husband and his ex-wife's parenting plan clearly outlines the holiday schedule: Basically we get the kids every holiday on alternating years—no exceptions, no questions asked.

If your husband is easily manipulated by his ex-wife and, like my husband, avoids conflict like the plague, you will need to do a little kind nudging in this area. First ask him to revisit the parenting plan with you (it is likely stuffed away in some file cabinet in his office). Read over the holiday guidelines together and discuss your individual expectations regarding custody during the holidays. Help him to understand that it is his legal right to have his kids on the holidays that are specified in the document. Bottom line, it is simply not fair to you or to the kids to give up important holidays because your husband is afraid to upset the applecart.

If you do not have a parenting plan or do not have holiday schedules outlined in the one you have, you need to remedy the situation. An official parenting plan can be created or altered with any divorce attorney and the divorced couple (ex-couple). While the experience in the short term may not be pleasant for your husband and his ex-wife, in the long run it will save on resentment, hurt feelings, and your own relationship with your husband and his kids.

Mother's Day: Your Day? Your Day!

Just so you know, there is a Stepmother's Day out there—another fabricated holiday mustered up so as not to confuse us with real mothers. I say harrumph to Stepmother's Day. If your husband and his kids can hardly remember Mother's Day, just think what they would do with Stepmother's Day. You clothe, feed, shuttle, and comfort them (when they let you). Thus, your stepchildren should celebrate you on Mother's Day. End of discussion!

The first time my husband and his kids forgot me on Mother's Day I was devastated. Despite my lack of training, I had spent the entire year being an exceptional stepmother. I was firm but kind, quick with a joke, and always prepared to make a bowl of nachos. I encouraged my husband to sign his oldest up for Little League. I scoured the neighborhood in the rain with my stepson for our lost cat. I taught both boys every word to every song on the soundtrack from *The Sound of Music*. I garnered great tickets to *The Nutcracker* (OK, so they hated it. It was the thought that counts). I taught them how to dance and to play "Chopsticks" on the piano. When it didn't occur to them to recognize me on Mother's Day I was shocked, but instead of dealing with it maturely, I bit my tongue and sulked in silence. When it happened again the next year, I let them know I was upset. I don't think they will ever forget me on Mother's Day again.

Now we have a standard Mother's Day routine in our household. It unfolds like this: At the beginning of May my younger stepson, Gavin, the outspoken one, usually announces from the barstool at the kitchen counter that he won't be giving me a gift on Mother's Day. "You know," he says, as if I am unaware, "you're not my mother." I give him my signature "stepmother stare" that means "You're buggin' me, kid," and then I inform him that since he isn't really my son, he should not expect a birthday gift from me. (His birthday lands in the same week as Mother's Day.)

Nothing is said again until the day before Mother's Day, just thirty minutes before closing time at our local mall. My husband mentions that he and his sons need to "run some errands." They return an hour later, brown paper bags in hand and smirks on their faces. They scamper upstairs to "discuss something important" and return with three wrapped presents and two cards. The next day, over a traditional breakfast of waffles and bacon, I open the overtaped, overribboned gifts to find a cat-shaped lawn ornament, an ice-cream scoop, and bath salts. I read both of their hand-picked hilariously juvenile cards aloud as Guy and Gavin roll on the carpet peeing their pants with gut-wrenching laughter. This is my Mother's Day moment, the one I cherish.

What About the Real Mother on Mother's Day?

On our second Mother's Day together, Mark took his sons to the store to buy their mother a gift—I found out about their little shopping trip about the same time I realized they had completely forgotten about me—again. I couldn't bring myself to understand how Mark could remember to shop for his ex-wife but completely overlook me. I felt rejected, a little jealous, and extremely insignificant. I handled the situation badly—stomping off and spewing expletives at my husband.

The question is not whether you believe children should acknowledge their moms on Mother's Day or not. The question is, should you and your husband be responsible for making sure his kids do so? Well, according to the stepmothers I talked to, the jury is still out. Many women believe that Mother's Day is her problem and that it's up to the kids to buy the necessary cards and gifts. Other stepmothers, however, have absolutely no problem taking their stepchildren to the mall to buy something thoughtful for their bio-mom. And others are perfectly fine with their husband's buying Mother's Day gifts for his ex-wife.

Jennifer, a stepmother of three boys, is very clear about where she stands on the issue. "When the boys were small, I always helped or offered to help them with gifts for their mother on Mother's Day, though I did not offer to pay. They could get gift money by 'working.' Once they had earned enough to buy something, I took them to the mall and helped them pick something out for her. And sometimes they wanted to make her something, in which case I usually helped them out. Now that they're older and have jobs, I let them manage it on their own. They rarely buy or make Mother's Day gifts for me, but they do give cards or call and wish me a happy Mother's Day."

Sassy Stepmother Straight Scoop

I have two rules on this. If your husband's ex-wife is married, technically her new husband should work with the kids to celebrate her. Your husband is no longer her husband, and he is not responsible for honoring any mothers except you and maybe his own mother. If your husband's ex-wife is not married or in a serious relationship, you should help your husband and the children decide on a Mother's Day present for her. Ask your husband to include you in the brainstorming and the shopping. That way the gift is from your new family rather than their old one, and you don't feel, like me, jealous or left out.

For those of you who would rather walk on hot coals than shop for a gift for the ex-wife, remember

this—your stepchildren may ask for help from their father in celebrating their mother on Mother's Day. If it
pains you more to get involved than to be out of the
loop, the proper response is a simple smile and a nod
and an afternoon out with your girlfriends.

Father's Day and His Birthday

I love celebrating my husband on Father's Day and his
birthday, particularly if it's on a weekend that we have the
kids. I plan secret-mission shopping trips with the boys
where we stealthily select the year's most desirable gift.
Last year's clandestine birthday gift was a pair of surfing
shorts. Mark doesn't surf, but according to Guy, he looks
"really cool" in them. For the last few years we've been
writing Dr. Seussian poems to go along with his gifts.

> *Oh, Dad, oh, Dad,*
> *O Dad-e-O*
> *You are the man*
> *Wherever you go*
> *You've got a great fastball and overhand throw*
> *Your pitch is great if you keep it down low . . .*

I always enjoy the bonding that goes on between my stepsons and me when we scheme and create poetry together.
Your stepchildren's mother may try to continue her
old tradition with her family, which might include cele-

brating your husband on Father's Day or his birthday as if they are still married. In the first few years of our courtship, my husband's ex-wife continued to give my husband (then my live-in boyfriend) gifts on his birthday and Father's Day. Her ostensible generosity was, in my mind, a form of relationship hijacking and a clear sign that she needed to be in control. Every time a gift or card showed up from her, I became purple with jealousy.

Janis, a stepmother with an inappropriately generous ex-wife, felt she had to nip the gift thing in the bud as soon as she and her husband got married. "When we were engaged my husband's ex-wife continued to give my husband gifts for birthdays and Father's Day. Some of the gifts were pretty benign, but others were completely unacceptable, like funny boxers and clothes. Since we weren't married, I just sort of kept my mouth shut, but once we tied the knot I completely nipped that problem in the bud. I basically told my husband that he needed to look the gift horse in the mouth and ask her to stop buying gifts for him like they were still married. She got the message and he hasn't gotten a gift from her since."

Sassy Stepmother Straight Scoop

Be sure to create your own Father's Day and birthday events and include your stepchildren in the planning. Do not be upstaged by the ex-wife. If your husband's ex-wife continues to give personal gifts to your husband on his birthday or Father's Day, lay down the law with your man. If it makes you feel squeamish, jealous, or threatened, let your husband know. Ask him to have a discussion with his ex-wife and to explain how unsettling these gifts can be for the family. Chances are, he will drag his feet on having the conversation at all, but when he finally does, you will be enormously relieved, and the ex-wife will begin to understand where the boundaries are in your new family.

Your Stepchildren's Birthdays

Not everyone has an ex-wife who wants to include the new wife in holiday celebrations. In fact your ex-wife, or should I say your husband's ex-wife, may think of you as the Antichrist and send you dagger-eyed stares when the two of you are in the same room. My friend Chris is not allowed to be in the car when her husband drops off his son at his ex-wife's house. If for some reason my friend is in the car, she has to duck because the ex-wife will come unglued if she sees her. This has been going on now for ten years. If this sounds familiar, it is highly unlikely that you will ever be breaking bread or throwing back cocktails at joint holiday parties.

For those of you who are friendly or civil with the ex-wife, at some point you will have to address the question, should you or shouldn't you celebrate your child's birthday as a clan—yours, mine, and ours? Be wary, my dear. I would rather streak around the block in a thong bikini than attend another birthday party with the entire bunch of us. We've tried it, and quite frankly it's not healthy—at least not for us. Someday I may change my mind, but for now our separate but equal birthday celebrations seem to work for everyone.

In the beginning, Mark's ex-wife pushed for the combined birthday celebration and we went along. Mark admitted that going to the party would be torture, but not going would make him feel worse. "What will the kids think if we don't show up to their party?" (I'm not convinced that kids think about adults at birthday parties unless, of course, the adult is carrying a cake with an obscene amount of frosting or a gigantic, brightly colored present.) Naturally I didn't have an acceptable answer to his question, so I agreed to go along. The last thing I wanted on my conscience was a seven-year-old boy's emotional scar. So I enthusiastically bit the bullet, bought a present, and put on a happy face. "Who knows?" I said to Mark. "It might be fun."

But my Suzy ChapStick approach was quickly thwarted when I realized that the entire guest list was made up of couples and their children who used to be great friends with Mark and his ex when they were married. I stuck out in the crowd of mommies and daddies like Courtney Love at a PTA meeting. Everyone seemed to be wearing some combination of hemp, Birkenstocks, wool socks, and baggy pants—comfortable Pacific Northwest parent clothes. I, on the other hand, was dressed for a party in my boot-cut jeans, Kenneth Cole boots, and appropriately sexy single-girl leather jacket. I have never felt so out of it, so self-centered and unmotherly. Friends of the divorced couple tried to include me, but clearly I was not one of them. But the worst part was the fact that the kids completely ignored me. My otherwise popular smiles and snickers were completely snubbed—I felt like a nobody. I wanted to instantly transport myself back to my old single life: lounging on my bed on a rainy afternoon, just me, my two cats, and a good book.

It took a few more awkward birthday parties until we learned our lesson. These days instead of combining parties, we celebrate separately. The kids usually have a big shindig at their mom's house with family and friends and then a little more intimate party at our house. The model works—at least for us.

Our birthday tradition starts with Mark's signature breakfast bonanza complete with waffles and syrup and continues through a day full of playing. At night we open the presents and have dinner at our favorite pizza and pasta joint. If the timing is right, we end the evening with a professional baseball game. And for the record, I dress in jeans and sneakers, appropriate fashion for a kid's birthday party!

Sassy Stepmother Straight Scoop

Combining birthdays with the "old family" is, in theory, a commendable idea, but not one that usually feels very good for the stepmother, who is trying to establish her footing as the matriarch of her own family. That said, I know many stepmothers who don't mind sharing the birthdays with their husband's ex.

If you're not one of these people, however, my advice is to be honest with the kids. Well before the big party at Mom's house, explain to your stepchild that you are sorry, but you and your husband will not be attending the bash. While you love her to pieces, it makes you and her father uncomfortable. Explain to her the two-party concept (two parties are always better than one) and that you would rather create your own birthday traditions at your house. The sooner you begin to separate these celebrations, the sooner your own family history will be solidified. You will be surprised at how quickly your stepchild or -children will adapt.

Your Birthday

If you're like me, your birthday is important to you. To make sure it's everything you hope it will be, create a verbal wish list for your husband and his children. I start a few months in advance, dropping comments such as "You know, what I'd really like for my birthday . . ." or "Hey, I've been thinking about what you guys could get me for my birthday . . ." I've been known to interrupt a sporting event by standing in front of the television, catalog in hand, and showing them the gardening tool kit I have my heart set on. I am also not above developing an itinerary for my birthday. "You know, I'd really like to go camping on my birthday weekend. Do you think we could arrange that? What do you say we make a camping reservation at . . . ?" While this may seem excruciatingly unromantic, I can guarantee that being forgotten on your birthday is ten times worse. And the good news is, once you start to plant these seeds, your family will start to remember the date on their own. Now, after several years of marriage, my husband is often the one who initiates a birthday conversation months in advance.

Christmas, Hanukkah, and Kwanzaa

"The first year we were together, Sam's ex-wife thought it would be a good idea if we got together for coffee and treats on Christmas morning," says Karen, a stepmother who learned the hard way that separate holidays are her preference. "It was civil, it was awkward, and it was, in my opinion, unnecessary. Having breakfast on my favorite day of the year at my husband's ex-wife's house (the one they bought and fixed up together) is not my idea of fun. If it were any other event, I would have done what I had always managed to do in uncomfortable situations. I would have escaped with a declaration of the stomach flu and a heartfelt apology to the hostess. Instead I bit my tongue, put on a grin, and wondered in silence who we were doing this for. I can't say the kids enjoyed it; they never looked at me. I know my husband hated it, and I certainly wasn't doing it for myself."

Sassy Stepmother Straight Scoop

You have every right to establish your own family's traditions on Christmas, Hanukkah, Kwanzaa, or any other holiday that you deem important. If you and your brood want to eat Chinese food on Christmas Eve and waffles at Hanukkah, it's completely up to you and no one else.

Our holiday tradition is about the same every year. We have a few Christmas parties in December, topping off the month with a big meal on Christmas Eve or Christmas Day (depending on the year), followed by a present-opening extravaganza and a walk in the park. We are in tight communication with Santa, so he knows which day to visit kids at our house and which day to visit the kids at their mom's.

As far as gifts go, Mark occasionally collaborates with his ex-wife in order to minimize the financial stress that holidays and birthdays can create. One year Guy wanted a Game Boy and several Game Boy games from Santa. In order to make good on his wish and to reduce the pecuniary impact of Christmas, Mark and his ex agreed that she would buy the Game Boy and Mark would buy the games. The group effort between the two households made buying the gift for Guy easier on both parents. When it comes to these important, financially stressful holidays, a little collaboration with the ex-wife can work, but make sure you have a celebration of your own, one that allows you to build your own special bond with your stepchildren.

The Ex-Wife and the Holidays— Gift? No Gift?

If you asked my husband to quote me on the subject of co-parenting or stepparenting, he would tell you that I sound like a broken record: "It's all so weird." It's my standard response to things that make me uncomfortable. Getting your husband's ex-wife a Christmas gift—now, that's weird.

Every year like clockwork Mark's ex-wife gives us a thoughtful Christmas present. One year it was a home-made music CD; the next year it was a batch of her signature cookie dough; the next year it was framed pictures of the kids. Each year the gifts are followed up with the requisite Christmas letter that she and her husband have penned for their close friends and family.

Mark, if left to his own devices, would not return the gesture and then feel terrible a month later when he realized that he "forgot to deal with it." For a while I was OK with that. But as the years passed I realized that Mark's ex-wife was a significant part of our lives, whether we liked it or not, and she should be acknowledged by us on Christmas Day. And so, given the fact that Mark is not one for remembering dates or for shopping, I am the one who figures out an appropriate gift. Several years ago I spent four hours editing photos of her boys and composing a photo album for her. It's so weird. But I must say, for us it is the right thing to do.

Sassy Stepmother Straight Scoop

When I told my girlfriend Tara about getting my husband's ex-wife a gift at Christmastime, she laughed.
"How do you do it? My husband's ex would fall down
with shock if we did something like that!" You've got to
do what's right for your family and for your specific
situation, but some words of advice to Tara and the
rest of you out there who can't stand your ex: Sometimes you have to take the high road whether you like it
or not. And like with all things, if you put out good
karma, eventually you will get it back.

Etiquette for Parents and In-laws on the Holidays

My friend Bridget, an animated schoolteacher and stepmother, finds her in-laws and parents to be egregiously
insensitive on holidays. "I have received exactly one
Mother's Day card from someone other than my husband
and kids," she rants, throwing her arms in the air. "The
card was from my brother's wife—not my mother, my sisters, or my in-laws. It's as if I'm not really a mother. If not
a mother, then what—an underpaid chef?" She pauses to
sip her wine and shake her head. "And my mother-in-law,
the holidays bring out the worst in her. Every year around
the first of December she gets this weepy, melancholy feeling for the ex-wife, Sharon. It's always, 'Sharon's alone

this year, and it must be so hard for Sharon now that you're married to Don. When are we going to spend some time with Sharon? What does Sharon think about that? Sharon used to do it this way. Blah, blah, blah.' Her bad manners are absolutely excruciating."

Another one of my stepmother friends, Rebekka, has a real beef with the fact that her parents do not send gifts to her two stepchildren on their birthdays or for Hanukkah. "OK, here's the deal," she says, pointing her finger at some imaginary parent. "Since I'm forty-two years old, my stepsons are probably going to be my only children, and yet when Hanukkah rolls around, my parents send my husband and me lavish gifts and nothing for the kids. While they're not 'blood grandkids,' they are still my kids. My sister's children get showered with gifts from Grandpa and Grandma. It's not fair. It makes me feel like I have a second-class family."

Sassy Stepmother Straight Scoop

Unfortunately, despite the fact that sixty percent of American families are in some sort of step situation, there is no official step etiquette. Those who aren't stepparents or stepchildren simply don't know the protocol for dealing with stepfamilies at the holidays. I believe that the only way to put an end to such outrageously hurtful behavior is to deal with it head-on. Talk to your mother-in-law. Tell her how the constant talk about the ex-wife makes you feel. Tell your parents that omitting your stepsons from the gift list makes you feel like an imposter, but even worse, it hurts the children. It's really up to you to help the people around you get it right. As trite as it might sound, the squeaky wheel gets the grease.

You don't have to be a stepmother scrooge at the holidays, but you do need to be strong and vocal about how you want them to unfold. Trust me, many of my stepmother friends laugh when they recall those first few dissatisfying holidays with their new families. With a few years under their belts, they have all learned to create traditions that work for them. With a little work and gentle persuasion, you can, too.

Nothing Vacation-like in a Family Vacation

The newly popular marketing term "family vacation" is an oxymoron. There is simply nothing vacation-like about flying the friendly skies flanked by two boys competitively pinging their Game Boys, or sharing a hotel room with two sunburned children, or refereeing a backseat wrestling match in a compact rental car in eighty-degree weather. No one knows this more than a brand-new stepmother who has traded in a week of her hard-earned vacation for a road trip to Disneyland, complete with farting contests, endless bickering, and the infamous nagging question, "Are we there yet?"

In my eight years with my husband we have been on

twelve vacations. Four of them were romantic getaways to Europe, Mexico, Hawaii, and San Diego, and eight were vacations to various locations with my husband's children—they are a blur. Let's just say that I have never needed a vacation more than the week following one with the kids.

One of the biggest challenges of spending all your vacation time with your husband and his kids is that you have no time alone with your husband. Basically you're expected to share him with his kids 24-7. If you have the kids only part-time and are used to being able to drop them off at school or their mother's house after a long weekend, you may find being with them nonstop for a week exhausting and somewhat disappointing. My friend Whitney, a stepmother of two children, recounts her own frustrations around this issue. "Our trip to Maui was a complete disappointment for me. We spent thousands of dollars on the trip, and I rarely got to see my husband. He was constantly entertaining the kids, while I sat in a beach chair reading alone and waiting for 'my turn.' Unfortunately I never got my turn and went home incredibly frustrated and resentful."

Most new stepmothers are guilty of planning their new family vacations with the same high expectations they had when they were single. They fantasize about the upcoming rendezvous, imagining themselves running on the beach with their husbands, skinny-dipping in the ocean, eating at fine restaurants, and getting drunk on mai tais. Some even go as far as to pack new lingerie. It's no wonder they're disappointed when they find themselves five thousand miles from home, eating dinner at McDonald's, and sleeping alongside an exhausted man who couldn't care less what they're wearing in bed.

Sassy Stepmother Straight Scoop

Kid vacations are not easy. I've been doing them for a long time, and no matter how prepared I am, I still have moments of vacation remorse. I fantasize about the day when my husband and I can jet off alone to some exotic locale and drink ourselves silly. For now, though, I just want to get through our kid vacations unscathed and, if I'm lucky, well rested. The following are some helpful hints from stepmothers who've been there. These gems of advice should come in handy the next time you find yourself planning a getaway with the whole family.

1. **Adjust Your Expectations:** The first rule of thumb when planning a family vacation is to adjust your expectations accordingly. Keep in mind, there is nothing about your old single-girl vacations that resembles those with your husband and kids. The two cannot, and do not, compare. Save your romantic fantasies for a later date and pack the practical pajama set instead of the naughty negligee.

2. **Keep Your Vacation Time Close to Your Vest:** Whatever you do, don't spend all your allotted vacation time with your husband *and* kids. Make sure you have at least two to three long-weekend getaways with your husband to make up for the lack of romance you have during your vacations with the kids. And don't be afraid to arrange some fun excursions with a few good girlfriends.

3. State Your Expectations and Find a Babysitter:
Before you make any plans to go anywhere, sit down
with your husband and state your expectations for the
week. If you expect to have some nice dinners out or
romantic walks on the beach, you will need to arrange
for a babysitter at the location. Most midrange to
high-end hotels and resorts can make these
arrangements for you ahead of time. Make sure your
husband is on board with the plan so when you break
the news to the kids that they're staying home with the
babysitter, he's not surprised or guilt-ridden.

4. Make Plans So You Don't Get Lonely: The
loneliness part of vacationing with a father and his
kids is a killer. I have two stepsons, which means that
no matter where we are, Hawaii or Syracuse, they are
going to want to throw the ball for a thousand hours
or forage in the forest for four-legged slithering
things. Neither of which I am interested in. A way to
avoid feeling like the odd woman out is to pick a
destination that has activities that interest all of you. I
prefer to book vacation spots based on access to spas,
yoga centers, interesting shopping venues, or art
museums. That way when the boys are off practicing
their soccer moves, I get to bask in a steam room,
shop my tail off, and take in some local color—that's
my idea of a good vacation.

Another way to handle the loneliness part of
vacationing with your husband and his kids is to go
with other families. My brother, for instance, is

married to a wonderful woman and they live in Hawaii. When we go to visit them, I get time to spend with her, shopping, hiking, and chatting, while the boys get to hang ten with their uncle, chase geckos, and collect bugs. The arrangement works wonderfully for all of us.

5. Take Turns Parenting: No matter how good your stepkids are, parenting for twenty-four hours, seven days a week, can be taxing on anyone. Make sure to take turns with your husband. Give each other a break to be alone. Split the day. You take the kids two hours in the morning. He takes them two hours in the afternoon. All the rest of the time is divided up as you like it. That way you both get some personal rest and relaxation.

6. Get Plenty of Elbow Room: Sharing a tight, confined space with two boys feels a whole lot more like torture than vacation, especially when you're paying a pretty penny for it. Be assured that once you've spent a week sharing a bathroom, tripping over dirty sneakers, and watching cartoons blare on a hotel room television, you will never do it again.

If you're planning a vacation with kids, do not get frugal when it comes to your hotel accommodations. Spend a little more money; get the adjoining rooms with a kitchenette and two bathrooms. Now is not the time to pinch pennies. Trust me, the extra money you spend will go a long way toward saving your sanity.

Places like Residence Inn or Marriott Suites are wonderful solutions for a family. They offer two rooms, two bathrooms, two televisions, and most important a bedroom door that locks.

Sassy Stepmother Cardinal Vacation Rule

Trading in your European getaways with friends or a week of hiking in the Canadian Rockies for the over-rated and misrepresented "family vacation" is not easy. Keep your expectations realistic and remember this Sassy Stepmother Cardinal Vacation Rule: For every one week you spend on vacation with your stepkids, you get 1.5 weeks of kid-free vacation in return. Now go forth and get that in writing.

CHAPTER EIGHT

Money Can't Buy You Love

Warning: Unless your husband or soon-to-be husband is the next Donald Trump, becoming a stepmother will probably do nothing for your pocketbook. It's not that stepmotherhood makes you poor; it's just that it may make you poorer than you were before you hitched your wagon to your husband and his tribe. Do the math. One income + one person = lots of fun. Two incomes + four people + an ex-wife + day care + groceries + college tuition + piano lessons = a different kind of fun.

I guess you could say that when it comes to finances I am pretty conservative if not paranoid. I was trained by my father, who was obsessed with making and having "enough" money, to believe that poverty was just a stone's throw away from our upper-middle-class, *Edward Scissorhands* cul-de-sac. "You can't rely on anyone but yourself for money," he'd say in a tone more appropriate for reprimands and laying down the law. "Don't expect anyone to take care of you. If you do, you may find yourself standing in line at a soup kitchen one day." In junior high my sisters and I lived in constant fear of becoming bag ladies and took it upon ourselves to start our own housecleaning and babysitting enterprise. My brother, no more confident of his ability to avoid hardship, launched his own moneymaking venture mowing lawns and pulling weeds. We were the only kids on our suburban block that cleaned the homes and weeded the gardens of our friends' parents.

My grandpa B., a second-generation Norwegian and Great Depression survivor, did nothing to relieve my childhood money anxieties. He regaled me with frightening bedtime stories that made Steinbeck's *The Grapes of Wrath* sound like a Disney movie. I was convinced at seven years old that avoiding abject poverty in my lifetime was a near impossibility. I was also certain, thanks to dear old Gramps, that my future was destined to include a freeloader lying on the couch, watching television and drinking beer. "You're a smart, hardworking girl, Sally. Some good-for-nothing guy is going to want to take advantage of you someday."

And then there were the social lessons my mother tried desperately to impart. "While your father and grandfather don't talk about anything else, it's important to know that in most circles talking about money is simply not polite," she implored, following one of my Dad's crass comments about the neighbor's new Mercedes. "Talking about money is as off-limits as discussing religion or politics. You just don't do it."

Given my background, it's no surprise that I nearly gagged on my own tongue when my Mark mentioned the three notorious and fateful words—***joint checking account***. By my reaction you would have thought he'd suggested we sell all our belongings and join a cult. I believe my response was, "What? Have you been smokin' crack?" In retrospect, there might have been a better way to begin our financial union.

Yours, Mine, and Ours— Learning to Share

I don't know about you, but when I was single I was pretty darn careful about my money. It wasn't that I had a lot of it, but I had enough to buy a condo, splurge on an occasional vacation, buy a few frivolous and overpriced items at Needless Markup, and still put a little away for retirement. If I wanted to forgo groceries for a week and dine on Cheerios and Top Ramen in order to afford a weekend getaway, I could. If my electricity bill was outrageous one month, I simply solved that problem by bundling up in blankets and drinking lots of tea the next. All my financial decisions and expenses were based on my actions alone. There was only one person to blame if my grocery allowance was spent in the Nordstrom shoe department.

But when my husband and his kids moved in with me, that drastically changed. Instead of my usual two hundred-dollar monthly grocery bill and the lonely cottage cheese container in the refrigerator, our first month's combined grocery bill came in at a whopping seven hundred dollars. I realized when I could no longer find the low-fat cottage cheese among the bottles of Gatorade, chicken pot pies, packages of bacon, jars of peanut butter, and vats of ice cream that managing the grocery spending in my household was no longer under my control. I saw instantly that feeding two growing boys and a strapping man was going to be a pricey proposition.

At the end of the month when it came time to pay our first month's bills, Mark sat at the kitchen table, calculator in one hand and a beer in the other, dividing the pile of envelopes in half. "OK," he said casually. "This shouldn't take long. Let's see, fifty-fifty. That means three hundred fifty dollars each for groceries. One fifty divided by two—that's seventy-five dollars each for water and electricity. . . ." He was right; it didn't take long—to see where he was going. "Hold on, buster, not so fast," I warned in my best *Cagney and Lacey* voice. "You want me to do what? Help pay for your kids' fruit roll-ups? I don't think so," I snapped. "This is how it will be, Mr. Man. I'll pay for the food I eat, the electricity I burn, and the hot water I use and that's it."

For the record I am not a stingy person; in fact many of my friends have gone as far as to call me generous. What bothered me most about the situation was the fact that Mark, without so much as checking in with me, just assumed that I would suddenly change the way I conducted my financial life and automatically belly up to the bar with my checkbook in hand, no questions asked. I suppose that, having just come off of a twelve-year relationship, he just assumed that we would pick up where he and his ex had left off—so much for assumptions.

It was only a matter of seconds before Mark realized that he had sorely misjudged the situation and the generosity of his paramour. Before he had the chance to respond to my objection, I grabbed the stack of bills and with a fine-tooth highlighter painstakingly analyzed every phone call, grocery purchase, and cable charge. "Now tell me, who do you know in the 714 area code?" It was downright silly. After four emotionally draining hours and a fierce argument, I ended up paying 40 percent of the mortgage, 25 percent of the grocery bills, and about 33.3 percent of the electricity bill (it's a hair dryer, hot-bath kind of thing). Mark begrudgingly paid for everything else plus child support payments and day care costs.

Our little system worked out well for me, except that at month's end I had lots of spending money and my prince in shining armor had about two cents rattling around in his pocket. It was frustrating. I wanted to go skiing on the weekends, but he couldn't go with me because he didn't have the dough. As disappointed as I was, I stood firm on my financial strategy, lest my grandfather suspect that I had fallen for a freeloader and his little brood. If I wanted to go skiing on the weekends, my only alternative was to go with my girlfriends instead. But carving turns on the slopes without him just wasn't the same. I missed him and felt heartless and guilty when I saw happy, healthy couples laughing and kissing on the chairlift. I wanted my honey to ski with me or take me to a movie or treat me to dinner, but after he had paid off all of his debts, he just didn't have anything left for us. If we wanted to do something fun, the tab was on me.

At the end of our first year together I realized that splitting our expenses based on the user fee system was just plain ridiculous. Scrutinizing the various bills and receipts required the accounting skills of an MIT graduate, the patience of a professional relationship counselor, the insensitivity of a heartless crab—none of which were readily available to us. It also became apparent that Mark, with his obsession with clean laundry and tidy bathrooms, wasn't the Al Bundy my grandfather had warned me of. Furthermore, by month twelve I was pretty smitten with his boys and was becoming quite a softy when it came to springing for new LEGOs or drumming up a whirlwind vacation to Disneyland. So without any prodding from Mark, I abandoned my hard-nosed attitude on the user fee system and uttered the words *joint checking account.* It would fund household expenses and child care costs. He would still be on the hook for child support and extracurricular activities.

After the first few years of sharing my life with my husband and his boys I became less concerned about "my" finances and more concerned about the overall health of our family. I came to the conclusion that unless I wanted to continue going on dates and vacations with my single girlfriends, it just didn't make sense to separate child support payments and after-school activities from our family budget. So at year four I finally stopped dragging my feet and suggested that we start splitting our finances fifty-fifty, all child care and support payments included. Though he never said anything to me, I imagine Mark let out a huge sigh of relief when I finally came to my senses.

You need not look beyond my Costco grocery cart, with its lifeboat-sized package of toilet paper and palette of chicken pot pies, to see that I am a changed woman since embracing my family financially. Our house is so jam-packed with groceries that if it weren't for the missing cash register and lottery kiosk, you might mistake it for the Korean deli around the corner. While my acceptance of buying all things in bulk is a profound transformation, I have found my biggest revelation to be the fact that I get more personal and spiritual satisfaction helping to support my stepchildren than I ever did buying a pair of new shoes. (By the way, did you know that you can buy 958 individually packed Go-GURTs for the same price as a pair of Jimmy Choo pumps?)

Sassy Stepmother Straight Scoop

I hope for your own sake and the sake of your husband that your baggage around money is a little lighter than mine. But whether money keeps you up at night or simply gives you a mild case of heartburn, you've probably at some point in your relationship felt petty, tightfisted, or taken advantage of when it came to helping to support your husband's family financially. If this is the case, you'll be comforted to know that you are not alone. According to stepmothers across the land, having to share money with their husband's kids and his ex-wife can make formerly generous single girls downright evil.

When you begin to ponder the possibility of com-
mingling funds with your husband, you may want to
take the following two important points into consideration. First of all, timing is everything. Getting married is a life-changing event, especially if it is your first
time. Add an ex-wife and children to the mix and you
have a change that makes menopause look like a day at
the spa. Why further complicate your life by trying to
overhaul your comfortable pecuniary patterns at the
same time you're learning to share a bathroom? In
other words, don't be pressured or coerced into
throwing all your money in one big pot the day after
you return from your honeymoon. Instead take some
time to get used to your new life as a wife and stepmother.

Second of all, don't allow yourself to be guilt-
ridden when you feel pangs of resentment at the very
mention of sharing your wealth. Every stepmother at
some point along the way feels stingy, resentful, and
selfish over the issue of sharing her hard-earned
money with people she hardly knows—it goes with the
territory, so don't beat yourself up. After all, it's not
every day that you decide to help support someone
else's children.

Learning to Talk About the M Word

Money—a five-letter word? The root of most marital spats? Maybe so, but it is a topic that absolutely must be discussed prior to getting married to your husband and his clan. No excuses. If you're like many other stepmothers, however, you'll likely avoid the discussion until you realize that your extra spending money is helping to fund the ex-wife's new Mercedes, child support, or private-school tuition. My advice? Get over it and openly discuss the *m* word long before you're too resentful to talk about it rationally.

"I didn't want to pry," says Marie, a smart career woman and stepmother of one child. "I knew my fiancé was financially stretched because I saw the pile of credit card bills he had stacked on his desk, and I occasionally heard him curse under his breath about paying his child support. But I just figured he had it under control. If he wanted me to know the gory details, he'd tell me."

After Marie married her husband, she discovered that he had thousands of dollars in child support back payments to his ex-wife and numerous debts that he and his ex had built up over the years. Suddenly Marie was more concerned about her own financial future than about hurting her husband's feelings or saying something inappropriate. "We fought like an old married couple the first year we were married—so much for the honeymoon period. I screamed at him and told him that he misled me. It was a terrible time. I would have felt so much better if we had talked about our collective financial picture before we got married."

Sassy Stepmother Straight Scoop

According to society's rules of etiquette, talking about money is "tacky." Apparently it is more dignified to silently go into debt or stick your head in the sand than to candidly discuss how much money you actually have or don't have. For stepmothers or soon-to-be stepmothers who are more concerned about being perceived as nosy or ill-mannered than about pushing for the truth, I have one thing to say. If you let your man's sensitivity or your mother's bygone social standards determine whether you go into your financial union with your eyes open or closed, you're headed for a frenzied first year. Money is a touchy and often delicate topic, but if you choose to skirt the issue rather than to discuss it with your mate, you may wake up one day to find that your eight steps to financial freedom have suddenly turned into a backward slide into financial ruin.

Men and Money

Many stepmothers report similar stories about sensitive husbands who are more inclined to dodge the topic of money than to openly and honestly discuss it. "He didn't want me going there," says Sandy, a newly married stepmother. "I tried to gently broach the subject, but he was just so sensitive about it. To him, it was a macho thing. I think he thought I'd leave him if I knew how poor he really was."

For most men, talking about money is akin to talking about size—to them it does matter. In our modern culture nothing spells masculine success like a fancy new car, a well-dressed wife, and smart, well-educated children. When a man can barely provide enough money for himself, his ex-wife, his children, and his new wife, however, masculine success is the last thing he feels. Instead of jetting around like a peacock in an overpriced Porsche, he's likely to be stressed-out about scraping together his half of the mortgage and worrying his new bride.

You would think, in these politically correct, postfeminist times, we would be a little more open to discussing money between the sexes. Unfortunately, however, men and women today still hold some very traditional views on who should bring home the bacon and who should be at home frying garden burgers up in the pan. This sexism around money further complicates the issue for stepmothers who feel awkward or somewhat inappropriate asserting their views on their collective finances with their husbands.

"Jim was so stubborn and evasive when it came to discussing money. He refused to clearly outline his monthly accounts payable and accounts receivable," says Jenny, a financially astute and somewhat outspoken stepmother. "I finally had to give him an ultimatum. I told him that if he couldn't be honest with me about his financial life, then I would have to call off our wedding."

The ultimatum worked and Jim sheepishly unveiled a complicated work sheet. Apparently he had a nice income on paper, but at the end of the month he was nearly broke because of all his financial commitments.

"Once it all sank in I realized that the only way we were going to make our union work was for me to help bail Jim out," says Jenny. "We created a strategy that allowed us to pay down his debt and build up our joint and individual savings and retirement accounts." Now several years later Jenny, her husband, and his kids all live a comfortable life. "I shudder to think what would have happened had I not demanded that original money conversation."

Sassy Stepmother Straight Scoop

Sometimes a cigar is just a cigar, but money is never just money. Money is society's yardstick to determine a person's strength or weakness, success or failure, power or influence. It's not surprising then that many divorced and financially strapped men just avoid talking about it altogether. When you marry a man, you marry his past, present, and future fiscal situation—there's no way around it—so it's best you understand what your economic outlook is going to be. Before you sign on the dotted line of your marriage license, make sure you take a peek at the columns on his financial spreadsheet and get the answers to the following important questions. If your husband tries to stick his head in the sand or tells you the answers to the questions are none of your business, kindly urge him to buck up and come clean with his financial background. After all, it's not only his ego that's at stake; it's your financial future, as well.

Questions to Ask Your Fiancé Before
You Walk Down the Aisle

1. What are your financial obligations to your ex-wife? Do you pay child support and alimony?

2. How often will the child support payments be revisited, and what is the likelihood of an increase or decrease in payments in the future?

3. Does your child support obligation end once the kids are eighteen years old or does it continue through college?

4. Other than child support and alimony, what are your monthly expenses for your children?

5. Have you had discussions with your ex-wife on educational expenses? Saving for college? If so, what was decided?

6. What about a will or a trust for the children? What are the financial plans for the children should something terrible happen to you?

7. When it comes to supporting your family, do you have financial expectations of me?

8. What are your financial expectations of me? College tuition? Groceries? Mortgage?

9. Do you have a retirement plan? If so, how much is in it? What are your plans to continue saving for retirement?

10. Can I please see your financial portfolio and your debt portfolio?

His, Hers, and Ours— Three-Account System

Every happy stepmother I have met in my travels has some kind of financial system that works for her family. Some women do not donate a stitch of their own money to their husband's clan, while others have completely signed over their paychecks to the good of their family. But one system that kept surfacing as the most liberating and livable was the *His-Hers-and-Ours Three-Account System.* While this financial structure may or may not work for your family, I think it is worth bringing up simply because those who have implemented it (or a version of it) feel tremendous equality, autonomy, and generosity around money. Here's how it works.

His:

This is your husband's own account that he pays into every month. The money in this account is earmarked for his spending money. He can spend freely on anything from extra presents for his kids to clothing for himself or beers after work with friends—no questions asked.

Hers:

This is your money. You put in the same amount your husband puts into his account and it covers everything from haircuts to movies to double nonfat lattes—no questions asked.

Ours:

This is your collective pot, made up of a predetermined portion of your incomes. The money in this shared pot goes toward your family expenses, like mortgage, groceries, vacations, child support, and school tuition. Nothing from this account is spent without the consent of both you and your husband. Any special payments for extracurricular activities must be agreed upon by both of you. No exceptions.

Sassy Stepmother Straight Scoop

Devising a financial system that works for you and your new family takes time and patience. There are many ways to skin the fiscal beast. You may find that you have to try a few monetary plans before you land on one that sticks. If you simply cannot find a financial structure that works for both you and your husband, you may want to consider enlisting assistance from a professional financial adviser. He or she can act as a neutral party to help set up a monetary strategy that you both can embrace and live with.

Money and the Ex-Wife

"It is one thing to agree to support your husband's children, but it's quite another to help support his ex-wife who doesn't work," says Terri, a stepmother who stood by

her husband for ten years while he battled with his ex-
wife, who was continually taking him to court for increases in child support and alimony. "Lucky for us, the
kids are eighteen now, so our financial obligations to her
are over."

Though it may sound shallow, how you feel about your
husband's ex-wife is likely influenced by her attitudes toward money and her ability to make a living. When you
find that your earnings are going to pay for the mortgage
and the groceries because your husband is paying his ex-
wife's living expenses, you are bound to feel some resentment toward her.

"It's not that my husband's ex-wife is nasty. She just
feels like she's entitled to my husband's money, which in
effect is mine, too, since we combine our incomes. Call me
crazy, but I have a difficult time reconciling why she gets to
stay at home while I slave away at my job trying to make
ends meet," says Robin, a corporate executive for a business consulting firm.

Other stepmothers complain that even though their
husbands give generous child support payments to their
ex-wives, the children show up in old, ill-fitting clothes.
"I'm not quite sure where the money goes," says Sandy.
"The kids, they show up like ragamuffins. In the divorce
contract it states that child support payments are intended
to cover living expenses. The last time I checked, that included clothes, too. I finally took it upon myself to buy
them a separate wardrobe that they wear at our house.
That way I don't have to run out and buy them something
new every time they show up."

Jane, a stepmother who works as a dental hygienist to

help support her husband's family, gets incensed when her husband's twelve-year-old daughter arrives from a week at her mother's house with clothes that are more expensive than her own. "I get so mad. Her mother spends money on her like she's a princess. The last time I saw her she had a purse that I am sure cost about two hundred dollars. I would never spend that much on myself, simply because I don't have the money."

Sara, a veteran stepmom who would rather chew on glass than write out a check to her husband's ex-wife for child support, gives this advice. "At a certain point you have to just accept the fact that you don't have control of the money once it leaves your hands. So instead of making yourself crazy, just pay the piper and move on. Besides, in the end it's only money. But there is one thing I demand for my own sanity. When it comes to writing checks to my husband's ex, I make him do it, even though I'm in charge of writing checks for our other monthly bills. It sounds like a small, insignificant thing, but it makes me feel less resentful and helps maintain my sanity."

Sassy Stepmother Straight Scoop

Here's the deal—the raw deal. Sharing your money with someone you barely know and may not even like sucks. Supporting someone else's frivolous lifestyle or paying for expenses that you don't think are necessary can be infuriating. Given that, you are going to have to, at some point, give in and stop protesting the inevitable monthly payment to your husband's ex-wife and kids.

Now, not every stepmother has to kick in to help support her husband's families (if this includes you, please go out and spend some money in honor of the rest of us). But for those of you who decide to give generously of your pocketbook, you will need to find a way to make the process palatable for you. Whether that means you divvy up the expenses with your husband so you never have to see the money slip from your checking account into hers, or your husband physically writes his ex-wife the checks from your joint account, or you have her monthly stipend wired into her account, it doesn't matter. As long as you set up an effective, emotionally neutral method that works for you.

You Said What?

Your husband and his ex-wife are bound to have discussions about money when you're not around. In fact you may prefer it that way. The problem with this arrangement is that ex-husbands often agree to their ex-wives' financial whims simply to avoid conflict. But it's a no-win battle when your husband comes home and drops the bomb that you suddenly owe a thousand dollars more in child expenses because of some star-studded basketball camp he agreed to send his son to. In such a case he should be prepared for a visit from your Evil Twin.

I've said this before and I will say it again for effect. Under no circumstances should agreements be made about shared household expenses without your approval. I guarantee, nothing will make you feel more hoodwinked, taken advantage of, or used than your husband and his ex deciding behind your back how your money will be spent.

His Kids and Your Money

Alexis, a stepmother who is continually trying to set the financial record straight with her two stepsons, laments, "My stepchildren always refer to our house, the one I pay half of the mortgage for, as 'Dad's house.' It drives me absolutely mad. They don't seem to grasp the fact that this house is half mine, too."

If I received a dollar every time I heard a version of Alexis's story, I'd be dressed head to toe in Prada. It's unfortunate, but oftentimes women who help to support their husband's first family don't get the credit they deserve. "I'm like the unsung benefactor," Alexis says sarcastically.

I've had similar frustrations with financial respect in our family, too. In the beginning of our relationship I found myself reminding my three-year-old stepson that I was the one responsible for the Friday night pizza dinners, the new SpongeBob SquarePants comforter on his bed, and the roof over his head. In retrospect, the fact that I was trying to explain the details of our complicated economic picture to a three-year-old boy who had just suffered the emotional trauma of his parent's divorce is embarrassing. But I felt like I needed him to know that I wasn't just a goofy playmate but a provider, too.

Now that the kids are older I have no problem correcting them when they say something like, "Dad said we can go to spring training this year." "Really?" I ask coyly. "Well, I'll just have to see if we have enough money to do that this year. You know, both your dad and I are responsible for our collective spending, so he'll have to discuss that with me before he makes you any promises." And when one of them slips and says "Dad's house" instead of "Dad and Sally's house" I understand that it is not an underhanded plot to make me feel unappreciated, but rather a shorthand explanation of his own personal geography.

Sassy Stepmother Straight Scoop

Feeling ignored or taken advantage of doesn't make anyone feel good. Especially if you find yourself slaving away at your job to make ends meet in your new blended family. While I don't recommend "Do you know where your bread's buttered?" finger-wagging lectures, I do recommend that you find a way to let your stepchildren know that you are contributing to their financial well-being. It's important that they respect your role as a provider; if they don't, it's quite

> possible that one day you will resent them and the money you contributed to raise them.

You're Driving What? When Financial Attitudes and Values Collide

Everyone comes into marriage with certain core values around money, which are usually passed down from one's parents (hence my fear of being poor). If you were raised in a financially strapped family, you may have anxiety about frivolous spending and are especially careful with your money. If you lived in the lap of luxury and are used to having money around at all times, you may be a little looser with what you have. Combining your hard-earned funds gets complicated when you and your spouse have opposing ideas and values around how your money should be allocated. It gets only trickier when you add into the mix an ex-wife who has her own ideas about how your husband's money (which is essentially yours, too, if you share expenses) should be spent.

No one knows this more than my frugal stepmother friend Marcy. One Friday afternoon after a particularly grueling week at work, she came home and was surprised to find her sixteen-year-old stepdaughter, Stephanie, at the kitchen counter eating chips and scanning the classified ads. Normally, getting Stephanie to read required a certain amount of arm-twisting or bribery. The fact that she had picked up a paper and was reading it without any prompting was downright remarkable.

"Whatcha reading?" Marcy asked as she poured herself a glass of wine.

"Car ads," Stephanie responded in a monotone voice without lifting an eye from the page.

"Really, are you thinking of buying a car?" Marcy asked, trying not to sound too curious.

"Uh-huh. My mom says I need a brand-new car, for safety reasons. You know, air bags and stuff."

"Oh, I see. What do you have in mind?"

"I da know. Maybe a Jeep or a Toyota 4Runner."

"Really?" Marcy responded, looking out at the driveway where her seven-year-old Honda with the two-year-old dent was parked. "Aren't those kind of expensive?"

"I guess. Thirty thousand dollars, somethin' like that."

"I see," said Marcy, raising one eyebrow. "Who's going to be paying for that?"

"Mom said that she and Dad would work it out, but that she wasn't letting me get behind a wheel unless it was new, big, and safe."

"Well, I'm not sure if your mom has just run into a pile of cash or what, but we cannot afford to pitch in for half of a Jeep or a Toyota 4Runner," said Marcy.

"Whateverrrrrrrrrr," said Stephanie indignantly.

At that point Marcy wanted to yank the paper out of Stephanie's hands and say, "Listen, missy—don't you know that whatever your dad decides to spend for your extra-safe car is going to come out of my pocket, too!" Thank God she didn't.

Marcy admitted to me that she and her husband could easily have replaced her old Honda years ago, but that she just didn't care that much about what she drove. "Cars don't matter to me. I don't want anything sexy or speedy. I just want a practical car that can get me from point A to point B safely. It just really bugged me that Stephanie believed that she needed something really nice. I guess you could say that her flippant attitude about a car went against my principal values around what makes a smart investment."

Sassy Stepmother Straight Scoop

Your husband and his ex may have different ideas from you about how to provide for the children. They may even try to compensate for unresolved guilt or to compete for their child's love by buying expensive gifts that none of you can practically afford. If you find yourself in this position, it is important that you state your point of view loud and clear; after all, they're talking about spending your money, too. If your husband and his ex insist on expenditures that you adamantly disagree with, you have every right to refuse to contribute. When my husband insisted that we get my oldest stepson a snowboard for Christmas one year, I put my foot down. Not only had we not budgeted for such an expensive gift, but Guy was growing so fast he wouldn't fit the snowboard the following year. I told Mark that if he wanted to do that for Guy, he'd have to do so with his own spending money. Eventually after much discussion we settled on a yearlong snowboard rental package instead. And the best part is, Guy didn't even know the difference.

It's Only Money

Just a couple of months ago one of my single girlfriends asked me how Mark and I handle our family finances (apparently no one told her that talking about money above a whisper and in public is taboo). I laughed a little because it brought back some painful and unpleasant memories about the long process we went through before we landed in a stable and loving financial situation. "We basically throw most of our money into one pot and pay all of our expenses out of that," I told her. "Wow," she said. "You're a better person than I could ever hope to be."

Helping to support your husband's first family is not about being a good or bad person. It's about building a family with clear intentions and proactively deciding what your role and contribution is going to be—financially and otherwise. It took me a very long time to see that "my money" was worth nothing if I couldn't share it with the people I loved most. It also took a while to understand that contributing to our family budget didn't mean that I was throwing my independence and power away. In fact it has been quite the opposite. I have found that sharing my entire life with my family, finances included, has made my life only richer in every way. Further evidence that money can buy you an enviable wardrobe, but it cannot buy you love.

CHAPTER NINE

What I Did for Love

In the first year of stepmotherhood I acquired an odd habit of conducting heart-to-heart talks with myself in the bathroom mirror. I would stop, stare at myself, and ask my reflection in my best Katie Couric voice, "Tell me again, why are you doing this?" I understand from speaking to stepmothers across the country that my "single girl within" bathroom banter is not all that unusual. Some stepmothers prefer having their one-on-one counseling sessions while driving alone in the comfort of their own cars. No matter where you have the conversation, you will eventually ask yourself—why?

The answer is pretty darn simple. It was love that got you here. Remember? The two of you could hardly keep your hands off one another. What's more, you were so head over heels for him that embracing his entire entourage seemed as painless as adopting his collection of black Aerosmith T-shirts and his tacky futon. It's not until you're well into your marriage that you realize that love steered you in a much more complicated direction than you ever imagined, and that taking on his first family is a far cry from embracing his high school wardrobe and sentimental knickknacks. No wonder you occasionally forget your original motivation for getting yourself in this step situation in the first place.

So don't be alarmed when you find yourself muttering to no one in particular and asking the question, "Why?" This temporary loss of memory is typical of early stepmother behavior and is usually an indication that you're lacking in the love, lust, or romance department—a problem that is usually remedied by a few nights alone with your man and a healthy romp in the hay.

Romance in the Real World

We women have been cursed. Ever since the invention of the fairy tale we have been brainwashed to think that wavy long hair, a tiny waist, and eternal romance was our God-given right. We were led to believe that one day a knight dressed in Armani would show up on our doorstep, gerbera daisies in hand, and sweep us off our feet in a brand new BMW (no baby seats included). And then we would ride off into the sunset with our Starbucks double two percent lattes in hand. The only problem is that the Brothers Grimm and their Hollywood protégés never told us what to expect after that. Many of us were left with the assumption that the fair young couple reached their castle in style and continued to stare into each other's eyes, paw at one another in public, and make love like rabbits. Can you say "farce"?

Unfortunately for me, I am one of those women who was raised on old movies and fairy tales. So it was a rude awakening when, on a dark and blustery December night, I finally came to the realization that life as a fledgling stepmother was more like a line from *A Christmas Story* than *Holiday Affair*.

My epiphany about stepmother romance happened not long after we had all moved in together. Mark and I had decided to take Guy and Gavin with us to a festive neighborhood Christmas bash. Giddy with delight, we drove to the party singing carols in a round—it was a scene straight out of some sappy Hallmark television movie. The show tune lover in me could not have been happier.

When we arrived, Guy's eyes nearly popped out of his head at the sight of the smorgasbord that lay before us. There were espresso brownies, mini-German-sausages, chips with dip, little quiches, baked Brie, See's candy, smoked salmon, chocolate-covered candy canes, pickles, sugar cookies, cheesy fondue, cups of rich eggnog, and boundless cans of soda in the cooler.

Mark tried to monitor Guy's intake, but quickly lost his determination when he realized that keeping him from the table would require a teeth-gnawing, arm-waving, foot-stomping six-year-old's scene. After mentally weighing his options, he reluctantly gave in and let Guy join the other six- and seven-year-old wolves as they stuffed their hungry little faces.

Several hours and several laps around the buffet later, we took the two comatose boys back home and tucked them into bed. Later that night I awoke to Guy patting my face and telling me, "I don't feel very good." Unsure exactly what that meant, I shook Mark awake and slid to the other side of the bed, covering my head and Victoria's Secret–clad body under the sheets.

Mark did what a parent is supposed to do when a child gets up in the middle of the night and complains of a stomachache. He took Guy into the bathroom, got him a glass of water, read him a book, and then put him back in the bed with his brother. By the time he came back to bed I was fast asleep.

Two hours later my beauty rest was again interrupted by a foreign noise coming from the boys' bedroom. The digital clock on the nightstand read five thirty a.m. Once again I shook Mark awake. "Something is going on in there," I said, pointing to the bedroom. Mark leaped like a superhero out of bed and flew into the bedroom where the boys were sleeping. Draped in a blanket, I tiptoed quietly behind him in anticipation of what I might see.

When he opened the door I saw Guy sitting on the bed à la Linda Blair, chocolate-brownie vomit spewing from his little mouth like a loaded machine gun. The entire room was covered in blasts of brownie spooge. I watched in amazement; I had never seen anything like it. All I could think was, "This is what they mean when they say 'projectile vomiting.'"

While I ducked for cover, Mark effortlessly scooped up both boys in his arms, one still vomiting and the other crying hysterically, and set them gently in the bathtub. Once he had them safely coddled in the bubbles of the bath, he went about changing the bed and washing down the walls.

I was absolutely no help. The unbearable stench, the crying boys, and the soiled bedroom were more than I could take. So I followed my instincts and quietly slipped out of my sexy nightie, pulled on my running tights, tied my sneakers, and ran for my life. An hour later, I returned, sweaty and relieved to find both boys fast asleep in a clean bedroom and my superhero fiancé dressed for work. Now, if that isn't romance, I don't know what is.

Sassy Stepmother Straight Scoop

I hate to be the one to break the news to you, but the story line of your life is not *When Harry Met Sally* or *Sleepless in Seattle,* and you are not Meg Ryan. Disappointing, isn't it? Romance, particularly for a stepmother, is not about lying on a blanket in the park and reading poetry to one another, or making passionate love on the kitchen table. OK, maybe your life was like that when you and your man first met, but I've got news for you—that can't last. Once the wedding is over and you ride off into the sunset, you will be faced with real life, complete with nighttime visitors, bodily fluids, and curfew patrol—which can be romantic in a spontaneous kind of way. So do yourself a favor and exorcise those fairy tales that were so carefully programmed into your brain, and get ready for romance like you've never imagined it.

Stepmother Sex

I don't know about you, but when I was single I had an in-frequent sex life. There were several times during my twenties and early thirties when I went so long between re-lationships that I could have easily reinstated my virgin status and talked my way into a convent. So when I met my husband and realized that he was "the one," I looked for-ward to the opportunity to make up for lost time. Even though my older sister warned that sex after marriage was less frequent, and my friends who were parents said that sex after kids was all but nonexistent, I was certain that that would not be our fate. I call that wishful thinking.

Ask any married person with kids, step or nonstep, about their sex lives and you will get blank stares, some rolled eyes, and a few "What sex life?" retorts. It is no se-cret that once a couple has kids, the passion they felt as newlyweds takes a backseat to more pressing issues like raising the children and making the mortgage payment. Indeed, most parents would agree that a house full of kids, a laundry room full of dirty clothes, and a stack of unpaid bills aren't much of an aphrodisiac. "Sex? Is that what you call it?" asks Penny, a mother of two kids. "I can't remem-ber the last time we actually had sex that lasted more than two minutes. If we get the chance to 'do it,' it's on the fly. In my book that's not sex—that's a quickie."

Many of my friends who got married young and had children late long for their honeymoon years before they had kids. "I love my kids," says my friend Lisa, a bio-mom who had a child with her husband after being married for seven years. "But I miss the relationship Jack and I had before the kids were born. Now we're so preoccupied with the day-to-day that sometimes we hardly have time to see one another until we flop into bed."

Alas, fledgling stepmothers do not have the luxury of the traditional "honeymoon period," free from child-rearing stresses. Instead they dive right in—to the deep end where they find that their romantic life is impacted by children, schedules, child support payments, and ex-wives. "Before we got married it was rare that I would spend the night at my husband's (then boyfriend's) house on a 'kids' night. I just didn't feel comfortable," says JoAnn, a new stepmother of two children, aged six and eight. "The only romantic life I knew with my husband was without kids. Once we got married and all moved in together, I had a rude awakening. On the weeks we had the kids there was no time for romance. Instead of wanting to cuddle and kiss like newlyweds, we had to attend to his kids, which meant we were shuttling, cooking, refereeing, and collapsing into bed at night."

Women who get married for the first time to a man with kids, unfortunately, are not granted the gushy, mushy first year of no-holds-barred heavy-petting, Sunday morning paper-reading, coffee-drinking romance that their kidless counterparts have. Instead they are forced to deal with issues that are more typical of couples who are several years into their marriage. "Sometimes I get resentful because I feel like I never had a 'newlywed stage,'" says Julie, a new stepmother and wife. "From the minute we came home from our honeymoon, we were knee-deep in homework, discipline, and a nagging ex-wife. Even though I knew what I was getting into, I imagined our first year of marriage to be much more romantic."

While you may not have the idyllic first year as a married couple, being a stepmother isn't all that bad. If you are part-time parents to your stepchildren (fifty percent custody or less), you have both your "kid days" and your "newlywed days," which allows you to fluctuate between protective parent and passionate paramour—a life that many of our married-with-kid friends envy. If you are a full-time stepmother, however, those newlywed days without kids will be few and far between, which means you will have to adjust your expectations for intimacy and work very hard to find the time to be alone with your groom.

Sassy Stepmother Straight Scoop

We all know that lustful sex is just one piece of the relationship pie and that living alongside your best friend and mate is much more enriching than simply doing the nasty. That said, your honeymoon year and the years that follow need not leave you wanting for more romance and intimacy. Just remember that keeping the marriage fires stoked with kids in the house will take lots of discipline, patience, and planning on your part—lest you get swallowed up in the day-to-day duties of raising children and running a household.

Tips for Keeping It Hot with Your Hubby

Here are some suggestions from my stepmother friends and me.

1. Schedule weekends away and alone with your husband at least once every few months.
2. Celebrate your month-iversary every month for the first year (if you got married on March 21, then the twenty-first day of every month is your month-iversary).
3. Don't expect much romance when the kids are with you; that way if you do get some action, you'll consider yourself lucky and not deprived.
4. Find some time every night to connect with your spouse. Make sure you have a consistent bedtime for the kids so you don't feel like you're on standby for your husband's attention. Once they're safely tucked in bed, take the time to be together even if it is only for thirty minutes.
5. Take advantage of your weekends or days without the children and act like newlyweds. "I remember a time when my husband put little yellow stickies all over the house telling me how much he loved me," says Nancy, a wife and stepmother. "That gesture got me through some otherwise tough times that weren't so romantic."
6. Vacations. OK, I've talked a bit about this already in chapter 7. Vacations with kids are hardly romantic,

even if you do go out of your way to schedule a few dinners for just you and your husband. If you want a romantic vacation with your paramour, go without the kids. Your husband, out of guilt, may reject the idea at first and suggest that the kids tag along. But after promises of all-night loving, moonlight skinny-dipping, snorkeling, and swimming with dolphins, he'll forget all about why he thought bringing the kids along was a good idea in the first place.

Schizophrenic Love Syndrome

"I didn't even recognize my husband when the kids showed up at our house," says Erin, a stepmother from New York. "Not only did he act like I was his roommate rather than his lover when the kids were around, but he got kind of mean to me. I literally began to wonder if he had split-personality issues."

Unfortunately Erin is not alone. Nearly every stepmother I have spoken with over the past year recounted a similar tale of schizophrenic love. It is so common that I have named the condition Schizophrenic Love Syndrome (aka SLS). If you're not familiar with SLS, you'll be relieved to know that you're not the one with the disorder; it's your husband. However, it is no less hurtful for you. SLS plagues divorced dads when their kids are around (this is not so much an issue with full-time stepmothers, who have their stepchildren over seventy percent of the time). Unfortunately for the new stepmother, there is no quick fix. SLS can be cured only with time, a little pain, and lots of discussion.

SLS usually flares up when your husband feels guilty about being apart from his kids and wants to make it up to them. When I first started dating Mark, I had a very difficult time adjusting to the behavior that stemmed from the guilt he felt about living separately from his children. When we were together he could hardly keep his hands off me, but the minute his kids showed up for the weekend I was all but forgotten. His boys seemed to sense his guilty conscience and demanded that he build life-sized LEGO rocket ships, play catch until his arm went numb, watch and recite story lines from famous Bugs Bunny cartoons, cut up their chicken, pour their juice, and be available for reading books at all times. They had absolutely no patience for their father's need to cuddle with me on the couch or his desire to scan the morning headlines. At the end of the weekend Mark was completely spent and he had absolutely no time for himself or for me. Ultimately the situation wasn't healthy for us or for the kids.

After several disappointing, confusing, and tearful weekends with the kids, we finally discussed his Dr. Jekyll and Mr. Hyde personality. Mark admitted that when his children came to stay with us, he felt like he needed to make up for lost time and give them his undivided attention. Though he didn't intentionally reject me, he often got so caught up in making his children happy that he simply forgot about me when they were around.

Eventually (it took at least two years), we worked through our on-again, off-again romance. I came to a point where I could anticipate his behavior in time to discuss it before the kids arrived. Once he became more aware of his guilt reflex, he was able to see it for what it was and became better at dividing up his time in a way that was healthier for everyone.

Sassy Stepmother Straight Scoop

SLS is a fact of life in a household with a dad who has only partial custody of his kids. Unfortunately, men have never been great multitaskers, and for them, sharing their love with their kids and their wife at the same time is like chewing gum, rubbing their belly, and walking a tightrope. While my husband is not perfect and I occasionally feel a little left out or hurt when the kids arrive and I fall off his radar, at least I know that his intentions are not malicious. Now if I see a weekend of "all boys, all the time" on the horizon, I make plans with my girlfriends and find other things to do for myself. That way, when I return to the house my husband is so excited to see an adult that he showers me with conversation and kisses.

Night Crawlers and Things That Go Bump in the Night

"I had visions of us having sex all the time once we were finally married. It never occurred to me that one day I would be afraid to run around my house naked for fear of being spotted by a preteen boy, or that I'd be sleeping in head-to-toe pajamas just in case a little someone found his way into our bed," says Alana, a new stepmother who has had many nocturnal visits from her stepchildren.

Night crawlers are the worst. If you don't know them,

they are the little worms who find their way into your bed around three a.m. They usually get there via a nightmare or a wet bed. They can kill an otherwise romantic night, make a grown woman feel extremely naked, or simply drive a girl from her own bed. "There is a whole world that unfolds in the middle of the night that I never knew about until I married my husband," says Alana. "I had heard the stories about newborn children waking at all hours, but I never imagined that I would be up at four a.m. washing the sheets of a five-year-old."

Because most single girls turned wives and stepmothers have no real-life experience raising children of their own, they come into marriages absolutely unprepared for sleepless nights and bedtime visitors. Out of pure optimism and ignorance, they doll up in slinky lingerie or opt for wearing nothing at all in hopes of burning up the sheets with their husbands. But instead of sparking flames, they find themselves rocked from their sleep by a little person who wants to slip in the sheets and snuggle.

Sassy Stepmother Straight Scoop

Lingerie and sex toys are nice, but you'll never be able to look your stepkids in the eye if they catch you performing for your husband in your favorite negligee and a feather boa. It takes only one time before a girl figures out that sleeping in the nude or dressing up like Nicole Kidman in *Moulin Rouge* is simply not practical with kids in the house. It's not that you can't have sex when the kids are sleeping in the room next to you; you'll just need to be a little more clandestine about it. And bear in mind, you never know what stories wind their way back to their mom's house. My advice? Get a good pair of pajamas and a reliable lock on your bedroom door. That way, there's no chance you'll get caught with your panties off.

Date Nights

When I was single I remember my married-with-kid friends talking about date nights. Secretly I thought it was a dumb phrase invented by aging yuppies who had nothing else to do but make their single friends feel bad about not having a date of their own. I couldn't wait for the day when I could finally "just say no" to dating. That's why I couldn't figure out why all my married-with-kid friends were dying to get back on the circuit with their men in tow.

"If we didn't have date nights, we probably wouldn't have sex, and we'd be so behind on pop culture that none of our single friends could stand us," says Reagan, a stepmother and new bio-mom. "I get so psyched for date nights that sometimes I get sweaty palms in anticipation of our Friday night rendezvous."

Another stepmother friend of mine who swears by date nights has some interesting rules about conducting oneself on a married date. "First of all, talking about the kids or his ex-wife is off-limits. Though I love his kids, the last thing I want to do is talk about his fourteen-year-old daughter's challenges in school over a romantic dinner. And talking about his frustrations with his ex-wife? Well, that's a surefire way to kill a date. It took my husband a while to catch on, but now he happily discusses other topics. (We do talk about the kids and the ex when we're not on dates.) It makes for a more well-rounded and interesting conversation and a date night that I can look forward to."

Now that I'm married with a houseful of kids every other week, I understand the concept of date nights, and I can't argue. It's a great idea. While it's not cheap, Mark and I make it a point to get a sitter at least two times a month so we can either go for a long walk, in-line skate in the park, or go out to a nice dinner. It allows us to be ourselves away from responsibilities and concerns and gives us a chance to laugh and have fun together like we did when we were dating. In the end, the time we have on our own together on those nights is worth every penny.

Sassy Stepmother Straight Scoop

Even though the concept sounds contrived, date nights are not a bad idea, particularly for a stepmother who needs a little romance refresher. So schedule it. Go see a movie, have some wine, and come home well after the sitter has put the little monsters or teenage malcontents to bed. Who knows? If you're lucky, you might even get a little.

Romance with an Ex-Wife Nearby

Conducting your relationship in front of the woman who once owned your husband's heart, shared his bed, and bore his first child is not something most new stepmothers get too excited about. Unfortunately it is the price you pay to be with a man who has kids. Certainly, life would be so much better if we could just stick our heads in the sand and ignore the fact that our husbands had sex with their ex-wives. But that's hard to do when you share a house with their child or children, who are living proof that they did "do it"—at least a few times.

"There have been times when I have wanted to march out every serious boyfriend I've ever had and force my husband to sit with each one of them for an hour or two at a PTA meeting or a sports banquet. Then he could see how painful and uncomfortable it is for me to engage with his ex-wife," says Mary Kate, a new stepmother and wife. "It makes me feel really strange to watch as my husband's ex-wife touches his arm affectionately or shares a private joke with him about their kids. If she were some casual girlfriend, it would be one thing, but they were married and intimate for a really long time. It makes me feel jealous and weird, like they had an affair or something. It's not logical, but that's how it makes me feel."

Eventually you are going to have to maturely face the fact that your husband and his ex-wife shared some intimate moments together, e.g., their wedding, their honeymoon, and childbirth. But facing the fact doesn't mean holding it against your husband or his ex-wife and giving them the cold shoulder when they are trying to be cordial to one another. If your husband and his ex-wife are trying to maintain an amicable relationship, there will be times when they may laugh and smile at one another just like regular people who know each other do. So don't let your imagination run away with you, and remember, you're the one with the ring on your finger and your husband in your bed.

TOO MUCH INFORMATION

"When my husband and I first started dating, I asked him all kinds of questions about his romantic life with his ex-wife," says new stepmother Lisa. "While I'm sure he held back a few things, I heard a lot. After we got married and I had to interact with her on a daily basis, I wished that I didn't know what I knew."

I'm the first person to want to do a little psychosexual analysis if given the opportunity, but I must caution you to quell your questions when it comes to the intimate details of your husband's other marriage. It's not like his quirky stories about the faceless, nameless college girlfriend who liked to yodel while making love. Though you may be tempted to ask about your husband's sex life with his ex-wife, trust me—what you hear will not make facing her at his kid's birthday party or bat mitzvah any easier. The less you know about your husband's romantic life before you hit the scene, the better. Save your sanity. Don't ask. Don't tell. And avoid the ex-wife who wants to share your husband's dirty secrets.

PDAs AND THE EX-WIFE

"There is something very strange about kissing my husband in front of his ex-wife," says Pam, an otherwise affectionate woman. "When all of us are in the same room—my husband, his kids, me, and the ex—it's really weird. My husband digs his hands into his pockets and I hang tightly on to my purse. It's as if we're being watched by this disapproving mother figure that we have to tiptoe around."

Some new stepmothers feel like an illicit girlfriend or an awkward teenager when they put their arm around their husband or playfully kiss him in front of his ex-wife. "I never feel like I can impulsively kiss him or hold his hand when his ex-wife and the kids are around," says Sara, a new wife and stepmother. "When it's just us and the kids it's fine, but for some reason when his ex-wife shows up, any public display of affection feels really strange for everyone. I actually think it hurts the kids' feelings to see us be affectionate in front of their mother. Maybe if she had her own husband, it wouldn't be so weird."

Not everyone feels as awkward about laying a wet one on their husband or playfully pinching him in front of the ex-wife. In fact several stepmothers told me that public displays of affection toward their husband helps to reinforce the fact that he's no longer attached to the ex. "Actually I don't mind flaunting our passion in front of her," says Laurie, a protective and self-proclaimed jealous stepmother. "It just further reinforces the fact that he's mine." Regardless of your comfort level with PDAs and the ex-wife, be assured that these awkward and possessive feelings are typical and temporary. Many stepmothers report that the weirdness fades after a few years of marriage and that after a while slipping a kiss in here and there in front of the ex-wife feels as harmless as checking the time.

Sassy Stepmother Straight Scoop

Loving someone with an ex-wife nearby is complicated—for everyone. The only thing that can make the situation more palatable is time, respect, and maturity. When you begin to feel jealous, awkward, or unsure about your husband's current relationship with his ex-wife, it's helpful to remember that your life will be easier if your husband and his ex-wife get along. And although they may have been intimate at one time, you're the one he whispers sweet nothings to now.

CHAPTER TEN

Going Bio

I love kids—always have. Ever since I was in grade school I dreamed of having a psychedelic school bus full of kids just like Shirley Partridge on *The Partridge Family*. It wasn't until my thirty-second birthday that I realized a bus full of my own was probably out of the question, and given my inability to meet the right guy, I'd be lucky to have one or two.

A year later when I met my husband, Mark, and learned that he had two kids of his own, I was silently relieved. I figured with his kids plus one or two of our own, we'd have enough to fill a VW van and take to the road.

On our first date I casually popped the question, "Are you interested in having more children?" Now, let's get something straight here. My husband is no dummy and can spot a trick question when he hears one ("Does this dress make me look fat?"). He knew by the tone of my seemingly innocuous question that his answer would greatly impact whether or not he would eventually get laid.

So naturally he said, "Absolutely, with the right woman I'd love to." With that, I mentally checked off the box in my brain that said "Will have kids." And that was the last we talked about it until a few weeks after we bought our new house and about one month before we got engaged.

I remember the conversation clearly. We were in the car. It was raining and I was driving. I was making a left turn onto the highway when Mark said, "By the way, I'm not sure I want to have any more kids." Stressed-out about more pressing issues, such as breaking the news to my dad that I had just bought a house with a man I wasn't married to, I conveniently shelved the topic, asking, "Can we talk about this later?"

Luckily for my husband, my first year of marriage and stepmotherhood was a blur. I was so busy getting used to the volume of laundry, dealing with the other woman, and managing my end of the car pool schedule that I hardly had time to ask myself the questions, "Have I been hood-winked by my husband?" and "How would I manage to find the time and energy to manage a child of my own anyway?" The more time I spent juggling the the day-to-day duties that go along with helping to raise two small children, the less enamored I was with the idea of having a bambino of my own.

And our friends with kids, well, they didn't make having a child sound like a bed of roses either. Like a broken record, they continually reminded us that our part-time-parent arrangement was a pretty good deal and was not to be taken for granted. They openly envied our biweekly Wednesday-through-Sunday-night schedule and regaled us with full-time-parent stories that made our hair curl.

It was true; our on-again, off-again responsibilities allowed us to schedule weekend getaways at the last minute, thrive in our careers, live like newlyweds, and be parents all in the same month—it was, ostensibly, the best of all worlds. Mark and I both knew that if we decided to spawn our own baby, our parental nirvana would come to a screeching halt.

After a few hard years of stepmotherhood under my belt I was able to finally ask myself the long avoided question: "Is stepmotherhood going to fulfill all your maternal desires?" No matter how much self-talk and scenario building I could muster, I kept coming back to "No." Mark's kids were great, but they had their own mother and didn't want another. It became very clear to me that if I wanted to become a certified mommy, I would have to have a child myself.

With my decision in the bag, the only thing that stood between me and my bundle of joy was a package of birth control pills and my husband. Flushing the pills down the toilet would be no problem, but getting Mark's buy-off wasn't going to be easy. And so I started to drop hints. "What do you suppose a child of ours would look like?" "When is it too old to have a baby?" "What are the genetic odds that a child of ours would have brown eyes?" My hints were always met with Mark's top six reasons why having a baby was not such a great idea. The list went something like this:

1. One more college tuition is going to kill us.
2. We'll never get to sleep in again for the rest of our lives.

3. You can just say good-bye to our spontaneous love life.

4. We're way too old. In fact we're so old we'll be an embarrassment to the child. She'll be defending us with, "No, they're not my grandparents. They're my parents."

5. No more real vacations, at least for another twenty years.

6. We'll get really fat because we won't be able to ride our bikes, ski, or hike the way we do now. Instead we'll just sit home watching Elmo videos and eating Ben & Jerry's ice cream.

His list rarely deviated until one day he ended his rant with, "But if you're just dying to do it, I guess we could." It wasn't the resounding support I was hoping for, but if I was going to wait for that, all my eggs would be dried up and there would be no baby to have. And so with his apathetic consent, I followed my heart, went off the pill, and threw caution to the wind. Within four months we were pregnant, and Mark and his boys could not have been happier.

Deciding to Go Biological

Let's be honest. The prospect of motherhood without stretch marks, swollen ankles, and a long sweaty labor sounds pretty darn appealing, doesn't it? If, however, you signed on for stepmotherhood thinking it would fulfill all your maternal desires without requiring you to lose your girlie elasticity, you best think again. I would stake a bet that if you are maternal at all, nothing will make you want a baby of your own more than being a part-time mother to someone else's kids.

Should you or shouldn't you? The decision to bring your own bio-child into the family isn't so simple, particularly when you already know, firsthand, how hard raising a child can be. But if your clock is ticking and your instincts are screaming, "I want my own," pay attention. Because if you don't, you may end up regretting your decision not to have a child and possibly resenting your husband and his family for the rest of your life.

Furthermore, bringing a new son or daughter into your clan can have a very positive effect on a stepfamily. "Having our daughter was the best thing we did. It totally solidified our family," says Bev, a stepmother of three boys and mother of one biological child. "My stepsons may not have been able to express love to me, but they do to their sister in such a phenomenal way. That love has gotten me through many days of wanting to choke the living daylights out of them."

"Having my daughter helped us to focus on shaping our family," says Jen, a stepmother of four kids. "It actually made me a better stepmother. I finally understand what it is like for my husband to feel so connected to his kids. That's not something a person can really learn without experiencing it for themselves. Now when he says he'd rather spend a Friday night with the kids eating popcorn and watching a video than going out with friends, I get it."

Bev and Jen are not alone; every stepmother I interviewed who has chosen to go biological reports that it's the best decision she's ever made, not only for herself, but for her family, as well.

Sassy Stepmother Straight Scoop

You may find that being a stepmother gives you just the right amount of motherhood you need. If that's the case, enjoy your part-time parent life and don't look back. On the other hand, if having a baby is one of your life's dreams, you should seriously consider it. But keep in mind, if you do decide to get knocked up, you will be well served to do so strategically (more on that later) because not only will having a newborn rock your world, but it will also rock the worlds of your husband, his kids, his ex-wife, and her new husband if she has one. And be aware that unlike first-time parents, who have a huge singular influence on their child, you will be raising your baby alongside siblings that aren't entirely under your jurisdiction.

A Few Good Reasons to Have Your Own Baby

I could give you a gazillion reasons why I think going biological is a grand idea, but you, my dear, are going to have to come up with your own list of pros and cons. After all, you're the one who may have to sell the idea to your husband. If you need to do some convincing, the following benefits may help you to state your case. If your husband is already on board and there is no need for a sales pitch, congratulations! Now get back on that horse!

1. BALANCE THE LOVE

"It just doesn't feel fair when my husband receives so much love and affection from his kids while I'm virtually ignored," says Susan, a stepmother of two kids, aged six and nine. "His kids literally climb all over him showering him with hugs and kisses while I just sit back and watch. The disparity makes me jealous and petty and I feel like I'm back in sixth grade trying to be liked by the popular girls. What I would give for one of my stepkids to spontaneously jump in my lap and give me a slobbery kiss. Instead I have to practically twist their arms to get a hug."

Nothing makes a stepmother feel more insignificant and left out than the sight of her husband being lovingly mauled by his kids. Particularly when the only affection she can consistently count on from her stepkids is the one their father painfully squeezes out of them.

"Come back here right now and give Sally a hug before you go to bed."

"Daaaaaddddd. Do I have to?"

"Listen—don't talk back to me. Give Sally a kiss—now!"

Call me crazy, but there's something about this picture that seems, ah, I don't know—a little insincere.

Many stepmothers tell similar heartbreaking stories of unrequited love. Their husbands get bombarded with affection and all they get are dirty dishes, a few loads of dirty laundry, and a stiff-armed embrace intended to pass for a heartfelt hug.

If you're hoping that one day your stepchildren will hang on to your pant leg for dear life the way they do their mom's and dad's, you might as well set up camp and wait, because with their mother in the picture it's simply not going to happen in this lifetime. The only way to get that kind of undying love from a child is to spawn one or adopt one of your own.

Terri, a stepmother and bio-mom, puts it this way. "Having my son definitely changed the love feng shui in our household. I used to feel like I was on an emotional roller coaster—just waiting for my stepchildren to show me a sign that they loved me. Now that I have my own son, my need to be loved by them has changed. I'm less dependent on them for day-to-day affections because I get that from my little guy. I know in my heart that my stepkids love me, but it's not the same way they love their own biological parents."

Sassy Stepmother Straight Scoop

When I started to write this chapter I asked my nine-year-old stepson, between commercial breaks of *The Simpsons,* for some input. "Gavin, do you think it's a good idea for a stepmother to have her own child?" I asked. He responded with an unequivocal, "Duh, of course." When I asked him to explain, he said, as if it were the most painfully obvious thing in the world, "Sal-eeeeeee. Euh, your own kid is going to love you waaaaaaayyyyyyyyy more than your stepkids will. It's just the way it is."

I could not have said it better. Having a baby of your own will change the love dynamic in your house. You will become so busy attending to the little one that you'll hardly notice who's loving whom. And your stepkids? They'll be relieved. No longer will they feel pressured to demonstratively deliver affection on command. Furthermore, it will give them the chance to get close to you in their own time and without coercion. As for your husband? Well, he'll just be glad to see you basking in the glow of a child's unconditional love.

2. BLOOD STATUS

Between friends, I must tell you that one of the most underrated and least talked-about benefits of going bio is your sudden improvement in rank—I call it Blood Status.

Before I had my son, Cam, I was positioned in my stepsons' minds somewhere between annoying older sister, bossy babysitter, and Dad's wife. The day after I spawned their little brother, however, that all seemed to change. The same boys who had relentlessly teased me like a sibling stared wide-eyed in respectful awe at the IV hooked up to my arm and the swaddled little monkey at my breast. Maybe it was my husband's colorful recount of the bloody C-section or the gruesome sight of me limping around the hospital in a cotton muumuu or simply the realization that their Martian-like brother came out of my swollen body that changed their attitude toward me. But suddenly, with a little medical intervention and a lot of drugs, I miraculously transformed from distant relative, once removed, to "our brother's mother." I call that Blood Status.

Another stepmother, Pat, says that giving birth improved her standing with her otherwise aloof and dismissive in-laws. "My husband's parents were not happy about my husband's divorce from his first wife. As a result they treated me like my husband's illicit girlfriend the entire first six years of our marriage. They used to ask me to take the family pictures at Sunday gatherings, never considering the fact that I wouldn't be in the picture. When I gave birth to my son and gave them a blood grandchild, that all changed. Now I am in all the pictures. Essentially my son gave me my ticket into the family—sick, I know, but it's the truth."

My friend Tara, a stepmother from Montana, was estranged from her stepdaughter Joyce for five years. But when Tara announced that she was pregnant, Joyce came back into the family. She began calling home more often and inquiring about the baby. And once the baby was born, Joyce came over three nights a week to care for the newborn. "It was strange," says Tara. "I think Joyce's way of apologizing for all the hurtful years of our life together was to come help me with the baby. Because of my daughter, she no longer treats me like an outsider but as an authentic family member."

Sassy Stepmother Straight Scoop

While having a biological child of your own will not do much for your short-term waistline, you can be assured that it will do wonders for your position in your husband's dynasty. Now, I'm not suggesting you go through nine months of morning sickness, water retention, and hemorrhoids simply to be given your own emotional parking space in your husband's family. But if you desire a child of your own and you decide to have one, an added benefit can be the sudden improvement in rank, from "Dad's wife" to "mother of my brother."

---

3. INSTA-SIBLINGS

All right, the cat's out of the bag—I'm an old broad. "How old?" you ask. Well, put it this way: I'll practically be dead when our son, Cam, gets married and has his own children. Given my aging ovaries and the fact that I had to strong-arm my husband to get him to agree to have another baby, it is highly unlikely that we will have another child anytime soon (barring a second Immaculate Conception of course). But that's fine by me, because my son still has two fantastic brothers, even though I didn't spawn them myself. And for that, I thank both my husband and his ex-wife, and of course the big stepmother in the sky.

Half, Whole—Who Cares?

Right before Cam was born Gavin asked, "Now tell me again. Is Cam really going to be my brother, or is he my stepbrother?" At seven years old he was having a hard time making the distinction between stepbrother, half brother, and plain brother. The harder Mark and I tried to explain the subtleties of modern brothering, the more confusing it became. Finally out of desperation to communicate, we turned to pen and paper and drew a very thorny family tree. Nice idea, but it still didn't make it any less complicated.

I was glad to discover that when our son was born, Gavin and his brother, Guy, gladly threw the semantics and titles, the "step's" and "half's," out the window and embraced their baby brother as if he were a hundred percent blood. With all the excitement and energy that comes with a newborn, they couldn't be bothered to make the distinction of what brand of brother he actually was. And to this day, quite frankly, I don't think they care. To all of them they are simply just brothers.

And for Cam? Well, as far as he's concerned he is darn lucky to have two strapping brothers who are, in his toddler mind, the equivalent of rock stars. And his older brothers are no less enamored of their very own, easily influenced, thirty-two-pound groupie.

In fact, next to attending a professional baseball game, there is nothing that makes my stepson Guy happier than parading around the neighborhood Little League dugout with his little brother Cam. Since he's been anointed the team mascot, one rub of Cam's newly shaved head between innings is believed to bring twelve preteen boys a lucky edge. Guy is undoubtedly the coolest kid on the team simply because of his connections to the budding Buddha.

Sassy Stepmother Straight Scoop

If you are like me and always dreamed of raising a school-bus-sized family but got started too late to have more than one child, built-in brothers and sisters can be a wonderful gift. I know for myself I never wanted to have an only child. I grew up with three siblings and wanted my son to have the camaraderie and chaos that comes with having brothers and sisters. The fact that my husband had two sons made all that possible.

My stepmother friend Beth had her daughter, Sara, when her stepdaughters were in college. "It was so amazing. I could not have asked for a better situation," says Beth. "My stepdaughters basically helped me raise Sara. They would come home for summers and holidays and want to spend all their time with her. It was like having built-in nannies. I feel so blessed that Sara has her sisters. I also know that if anything ever happens to me, she will be in good hands."

4. THERE IS NOTHING BETTER THAN A DADDY DOULA

I am proud to say that when it comes to handling a newborn, my husband can go head-to-head anywhere, anytime, with a seasoned doula or an overprotective mother-in-law. I don't mean to brag, but he can literally change a dirty diaper, dispose of it in the Genie, and tidy up the changing table in the same amount of time it takes most new dads to discover that their child needs changing. And if you think that's good, he can also balance a sleeping baby on his shoulder, warm up milk, and get a pot of coffee brewing in under three minutes flat. Now, if you ask me, that's not only studly—it's romantic!

"I was an extremely calm mother, largely because I had an experienced dad by my side interpreting all the strange baby sounds and colors that were coming out of my son's body," says Renee. "My first-time-parent friends, however, spent their first six months of motherhood in a constant state of paranoia. I just remember my husband saying, 'Don't worry. It's all very normal and it's temporary.' It was like having a personal shrink on hand at all times."

Sassy Stepmother Straight Scoop

Taking care of an infant the size of a small cat can be pretty horrifying, particularly when you haven't changed a diaper since you swore off babysitting in high school. And no matter how much time you spent diapering a plastic baby doll in birthing classes, nothing can quite prepare you for the real thing. That's why having an experienced mate who can show you how to install a car seat, pack a diaper bag, draw a bath, heat a bottle, burp the babe, and take a temperature can be such a blessing. Just don't go bragging about it to any first-time mothers. If you do, they'll be calling your very own Dr. Spock at all hours of the night.

5. IRREVOCABLE MEMBERSHIP
TO THE MOMMY CLUB

Once you have your own baby you will automatically be considered a lifetime member of the Mommy Club (if you've skipped ahead, you may want to brush up on the Mommy Club basics in chapter 2). And once you're in, all the seemingly inappropriate and unappetizing mumbo jumbo that once made your head spin will suddenly start to mean something to you. Before you know it you'll be talking amniocentesis, vaginal birth, leaky breasts, umbilical cord, broken water, and incontinence as if it were your first language.

Just last week I was reminded of how intimate and exclusive the Mommy Club can be. I was at a Starbucks ordering my usual tall nonfat latte when I heard a woman standing in line behind me say the word "vaginally." Not sure if I was hearing correctly, I turned to see who might be brave enough to say such a word out loud and in mixed company. I saw, to my surprise, a well-dressed thirtyish woman holding a small baby on her hip talking to a very pregnant woman at the end of the line.

"Are you going to have it vaginally?" she asked again, as if it were just the two of them in the entire place. Her friend, the pregnant one at the very end of the line, answered loud enough to be heard over the din of the coffee shop, "No—I have placenta previa," and pointed to somewhere between her big belly and her crotch. "Basically my placenta is covering my birth canal, so I have to have a scheduled C-section." With that, she mimed over her black pregnancy pants a knife cutting through her pubic line.

The men in line all looked at the ground while the

nonmothers looked on appalled (just as I would have two years ago). The rest of the women in line seemed unfazed—probably mothers themselves. This kind of conversation, while shocking to the uninitiated, is typical of women in the Mommy Club. See what you have to look forward to?

Sassy Stepmother Straight Scoop

Being a lifetime member of the Mommy Club comes with a multitude of benefits, including but not limited to the license to engage in otherwise shocking conversations. But don't go joining the ranks just so you can surprise strangers in public places with the *v* word. Believe it or not, there are other benefits that you might find more compelling. Like the whole new gaggle of "mommy" friends you'll find when you hit the streets with your state-of-the-art stroller. And don't be surprised or offended when the same women who barely gave you the time of day when you were simply a step-mom take great interest in you all of a sudden. Just smile and accept it. No new mommy should turn down the camaraderie of another mother.

---

6. A FRESH PERSPECTIVE ON THE EX

Having a baby of your own can turn your world upside down, so much so that you may start to feel some empathy and respect for your husband's ex-wife.

"Once I had my baby I was able to put myself in her

shoes," says Sandra, a stepmother turned bio-mom. "When my husband's ex asked me if she could hold my newborn, I froze. Finally I understood firsthand what she must have felt when she had to hand over her own flesh and blood to me for an entire weekend."

Other stepmothers report that the things that used to bug the living daylights out of them about their husband's ex-wife suddenly become nonissues once they have their own baby. "I stopped focusing on the little stuff that used to bug me so much about her, like the incessant fussing over the kids or the phone calls that followed a drop-off," says Renee, another stepmother with her own children. "I am certain that had I been in her shoes, I would have done the same thing. I might have even been a little more obnoxious. I guess I wouldn't have that insight if I didn't have my own baby to fuss over now."

"Discipline was always a hot point for me," says April, a stepmom turned bio-mom. "Before I had my own baby I couldn't understand why my stepkids' mother was so lax with them on discipline. I remember criticizing her style and making comments like 'Why does she let them get away with having messy rooms?' Now that I have my own baby, I understand that it's not always easy to do the right thing. Sometimes you just fold because it's less stressful than the alternative."

Sassy Stepmother Straight Scoop

Empathy can go a long way in creating a respectful relationship between a stepmother and a bio-mom.

> While you may never be great friends with your husband's ex, having your own baby can at least allow you to see the world through her eyes now and then, which isn't such a bad thing.

The Practicalities of Going Bio

Now that I've told you all the glorious reasons why having a bio-babe is a good thing, let me tell you that it's not without its complications. There are practical matters to consider (such a wet blanket!). But if you heed the following sensible stepmotherly advice, you will find that bringing a baby into your multilayered family can go quite swimmingly. If you decide to simply ignore it and throw caution to the wind, you may be forced to dog-paddle in very rough seas. I don't know about you, but I'd rather do the sidestroke than dog-paddle any day.

A Husband on the Fence

So you've decided that having your own baby is a good idea, but your husband's on the fence. What do you do? Many divorced men, strapped with the financial and emotional complications that go along with part-time parenting, are not chomping at the bit to have more kids. That doesn't mean that he won't agree to have one or two more; it just means your sales job is going to be a little more challenging.

When I was deciding whether or not to have a child of my own, I consulted Jan, a stepmother friend of mine who had just given birth to her own son (her stepson was eighteen years old at the time). When I asked her if her husband had supported her decision to have another child, she said, "What are you, kidding? No man who has been divorced and lived through financial hardship raising a child is going to jump up and down at the idea of having another one. Especially if he's over forty. If you wait for him to jump with joy at the idea, you'll be waiting for the rest of your life. If you really want a baby, then you should do it. He'll come along. If he is a good father to his other kids, he'll be a great father to this one, too. Trust me."

Sassy Stepmother Straight Scoop

Jan's advice was sound. I have since heard from many stepmothers that their children were conceived while their husbands were dragging their feet (apparently it has no effect on sperm count). But once the pregnancy was a reality, the same lukewarm men became giddy with delight. "My husband is so crazy about Nora, our daughter," says Jennifer, a bio-mom with stepchildren. "You would have thought it was all his idea. I don't dare remind him that the only reason why we have her is because I didn't let him talk me out of it."

Breaking the News to the Kids

When you find out you're pregnant, you're going to be pretty darn excited. You'll probably want to run around the neighborhood telling anyone who will listen that you are, in fact, with child. Keep in mind, however, that breaking the news to your stepchildren without preparation can be pretty surprising and threatening for them. In fact, if it's the first they've heard of it, they will be so preoccupied with how a baby might affect their own standing in the family that they're unlikely to mirror your enthusiasm.

"When we told my stepson, Jack, that he was going to have a sister, he ran into his bedroom and slammed the door," says Jackie, a sassy stepmother who decided to go bio. "My husband and I were so excited to tell him. We thought he'd be happy about it. As it turned out he had some real concerns about losing his status as the only child."

Children who see their fathers only a few times a year may have a harder time with the news of a new family member. Erin, a stepmother and new bio-mom, recounts the telephone conversation she and her husband had with her stepdaughter. "Jenny lives halfway across the country from us, so we decided to call her with the news. She didn't sound terribly excited about it, but I just chalked that up to the fact that she had just turned thirteen. A few weeks later she called her dad crying. She asked him, between sobs, if he still wanted her to come out every summer, even though he'd have another family."

The prospect of having a needy baby in the house can be threatening for a child. After all, no one wants to be upstaged by a seven- or eight pound gurgling infant. Kids worry about things such as "Will our house suddenly smell like dirty diapers?" or "Will my stepmother love me less when she has her own baby?" or "Will I have to share my dad?" It's natural for kids to worry about how another child in the family will affect them, particularly when their time with their dad is limited in the first place.

Sassy Stepmother Straight Scoop

Instead of spontaneously announcing that you have a bun in the oven, begin to plant the idea in your stepkids' brain long before you get pregnant. Try something as simple as "Hey, what would you think if we had another brother or sister?" Rhetorical questions like this can provoke a child's anxieties or fears and give you time to address them before you're preoccupied with ultrasounds and morning sickness.

In our case we began to consider a baby out loud when we moved to a new house. I would say things to my stepsons such as "We need a bigger house just in case we decide that we need another brother or sister." Or "If we had another little brother, what do you think he would look like?" Or "Hey, if we had another brother or sister, what do think we would name them?" When we finally announced months later that we were pregnant, the kids were very excited and far from surprised.

Timing Is Everything

If you do decide to have children of your own, something you may want to consider is timing. While you're not getting any younger, neither are your stepkids, which can be a good thing. Most of the women I spoke with found that older siblings (six or seven years old and up) were far easier to deal with than younger stepchildren at the time of their pregnancies. Technically, the older the stepchild, the more mature he or she will be about gaining a new family member (there are exceptions here). I know in my specific case my stepsons, who were seven and eleven at the time of their brother's birth, could not have been happier with the idea of having a baby brother. At that point we had all been living together for five years, which was enough time for them to get used to me. As a result we never had to deal with weird jealousies or unexpected tantrums. And as an added bonus they were old enough to help me out with the baby.

Sassy Stepmother Straight Scoop

While timing is everything, you can't exactly ask Mother Nature to give you preferential treatment simply because you want a built-in babysitter. If you get pregnant with a four- or five-year-old stepchild in the house, you'll get through it. It just won't be as easy as if he or she were, say, ten to fourteen years old. "It is so great," says Amy, a stepmother of two children, ages twelve and sixteen. My stepchildren are so entertained by my son, and he has never been wanting for attention. They practically want to pay me so they can babysit."

A Family Affair

My pregnancy was wonderful, and I'm not one of those sentimental women who thought being big, fat, and plagued with heartburn was beautiful. It was wonderful because I got to share it with three very excited and playful guys. It was a veritable guessing game the entire nine months. It started out, "Do you think it's going to be a boy or a girl?" We all placed bets and debated the possibility of having a sister in the house. Once we knew that the baby was going to be a brother, we wagered on the due date, length, weight, and eye color. My oldest stepson, a budding statistician, created a chart to document our individual hypotheses. It was great fun until they started speculating about my weight gain and stomach circumference. At that point I decided to distract them with the name game. We spent three months contemplating, arguing about, and deliberating all the variations on names. Every day my youngest stepson would come home with another idea. "How about Carter? Carson? Ian or Fred?" Finally we all agreed on Cam. By the time Cam was born, we all felt like we had known him for a very long time.

"I loved getting my husband's kids involved in my pregnancy," says Amy. "They were so supportive and fun. They kept asking me, 'How many more days left?' The closer we got to the due date, the more excited they got. It just wouldn't have been as fun without them."

Sassy Stepmother Straight Scoop

Having a baby can be exciting for a family, especially for siblings—of any age. The more you can include your stepchild or -children in your pregnancy, the more vested and prepared they will be when the newborn arrives. Ask your stepchildren for their suggestions on names, paint colors, and baby clothes. Show them the ultrasound video. Get them involved in decorating the nursery or assembling the changing table. You'll be surprised not only at how helpful they can be but also at how much you will bond during the process.

Who Comes to the Hospital?

For the record I am a modest person and am not entirely comfortable being buck naked in front of anyone other than my husband. And then I prefer the lights to be low. While I'm not here to judge people who videotape their labor, I must admit it's not for me. That said, there are several stepmothers I know who not only videotaped the birth of their baby but invited their stepchildren to the show. I have no advice on this—you do what's comfortable for you.

I had a planned C-section due to some complications, so luckily for me there was no chance of unexpected guests or videographers. We had the baby around six p.m. and the boys showed up the next morning around nine a.m. When they arrived we had little gifts for them from their new brother, Cam, and they in turn had gifts for him. That night they went home with their dad while I stayed in the hospital and bonded with their new brother. The boys continued to come back to the hospital every day until I returned home with the baby. The next day, thanks to their mom, they left for a two-week vacation so we could adjust to sleepless nights and endless loads of laundry without the hassles of carpooling and curfews.

My friend Lynn, who had to be in the hospital for two weeks leading up to the birth of her son, saw her husband's ex-wife and her stepson every day that she was in the hospital. "It was kind of weird," says Lynn. "She came every day with my stepson, Jason, to visit us. She brought gifts and coffee every time she came. It was sweet and definitely odd at the same time."

Sassy Stepmother Straight Scoop

Regardless of where you fall on the modesty meter, you get the final call on who comes to the hospital and when. Make sure you discuss the details with your husband and his kids beforehand so there are no surprises. Also, if you have a loose and somewhat friendly relationship with your husband's ex, be sure to let her know whether or not it is appropriate for her to visit you in the hospital. After all, the last thing you want is

a perky ex-wife surprising you when you feel and look
like you've just been through the wringer.

Can Baby Come Stay at My Mom's House?

My stepson asked me recently, "Is my mom Cam's stepmom?" While I wanted to scream, "NO," I calmly replied,
"No, she's not really related to him."

He sat silent for a few minutes and then asked, "How
come?"

"Because she isn't anyone to him. She's just your mother
and no one else's mother," I explained.

"But she's a stepmom to my stepbrothers and -sister."

"Yes, well, that's because she married their father."

"Yeah, but you married her old husband, so doesn't
that make Cam something to her?"

The circuitous conversation went on like a never end-
ing record until I finally agreed that his mother was, in
fact, sort of related to my son Cam.

It was shortly thereafter that he asked, "Can Cam come to
my mom's house sometime?" I almost gagged before I could
utter the words, "Ah, ummm, well. Hmmm. We'll see."

My friend Peggy has absolutely no issues with letting
her three-year-old daughter, Amanda, stay overnight
with her half sister at her mom's house. "I figure that
there probably is no better babysitter in the world than my

husband's ex-wife. She loves Amanda and really values the relationship her own daughter has with her little sister. I feel perfectly comfortable sending her over for the night while my husband and I go out with friends."

That's a little too close for comfort for me, but I have met several stepmothers who feel exactly the same way about leaving their children with their husband's ex-wife. I guess all I can say to that is, don't look a gift horse in the mouth and never say never.

Sassy Stepmother Straight Scoop

If you think that having your own child will further distance you from your husband's ex-wife, you will be absolutely dumbstruck when your stepchild invites your bio-child home to his mother's house for the weekend, or heaven forbid, the ex asks if she can hold him. In such instances your instincts may tell you to run for cover, bare your incisors, or simply circle the den, none of which will make you look very good, or reasonable for that matter.

If your husband's ex-wife asks if she can hold your baby, by all means let her (barring the possibility that she is a raving lunatic). After all, you held her babies or comforted her teenagers and you didn't even have to ask.

Regarding weekend visits to the ex's house, well, that's a tough one. Stepmothers I have spoken to are all

The Single Girl's Guide...

over the board when it comes to sharing their offspring with their stepchildren's mother. Do what you are comfortable with. But make sure that if you decide not to allow it, you do so with the utmost respect and grace.

228

Long Live the Stepmother

A couple of weeks ago while catching up with some girlfriends over margaritas and appetizers, I realized something profound—I like the word "stepmother." It's efficient. Not only does it roll melodically off my tongue, but it does a great job of explaining the relationship a person has in a family, just as the words "mother," "daughter," and "milkman" do.

My word-loving insight occurred when my friend Ann, a new wife and stepmother, regaled us with stories of her first few months of marriage and stepmotherhood. She told the gaggle of chatty comrades in a hushed voice reserved for salacious gossip, "In my family we don't use the word 'step.'"

"Huh? What exactly do you call yourself, then?" I pried. "And what exactly does your stepdaughter call you?"

"Well, we just use the term 'other mother,'" she said as

if the words "other mother" offered her more clout in the realm of alternative families than the word "stepmother" ever could.

"Hold on. Wait a second here," I said. "So when some kid points to you and asks your stepdaughter, 'Who's that?' do you think she'll say, 'That's my other mother'?"

"Yeah, that's the thinking."

"Do you think your stepdaughter's friends will know what 'other mother' means? Maybe they'll think your stepdaughter has two lesbian mothers. Not that there is anything wrong with that."

While the rest of the women at the table laughed at my joke, Ann looked stymied, as if she hadn't entertained the possibility of being seen as one of two mothers in the same household. After a second or two she came back with: "Well, I've always been a little out there, so being confused with a lesbian works for me."

"But being confused with a stepmother doesn't? What's up with that?" I asked.

"Sally, you're like the Norma Rae of stepmothers," said Jackie, another friend at the table. Everyone laughed.

"At least I'm not in the closet about being a step-mother," I snapped.

I drove home that night a little buzzed and very bugged by Ann's need to be something other than a stepmother. I felt like she was some kind of New Age antifeminist femi-nist in a sea of authentic, hardworking bra burners. I wondered, was Ann protecting herself from the step-mother stereotype or her four-year-old stepdaughter? If she was worried about her stepdaughter, she need not waste the energy because her generation doesn't carry the

Estess, Patricia Schiff. *Money Advice for Your Successful Remarriage: Handling Delicate Financial Issues Intelligently and Lovingly.* ASJA Press, 2001.

Goodman, Karon Phillips. *The Stepmom's Guide to Simplifying Your Life.* Equilibrium Press, 2002.

Keenan, Barbara Mullen. *When You Marry a Man with Children: How to Put Your Marriage First and Stay in Love.* Pocket, 1992.

Millian, Lenore Fogelson, and Stephen Jerry Millian. *The Second Wives Club: Secrets for Becoming Lovers for Life.* Beyond Words, 1999.

Mulford, Philippa Greene. *Keys to Successful Stepmothering.* Barron's, 1996.

Norwood, Perdita Kirkness, and Teri Wingender. *The Enlightened Stepmother, Revolutionizing the Role.* Avon, 1999.

NEWLYWED ADVICE BOOKS

Bliss, Sara. *The Thoroughly Modern Married Girl: Staying Sensational After Saying "I Do."* Broadway Books, 2003.

Bourland, Julia. *Hitched: The Go-Girl Guide to the First Year of Marriage.* Atria Books, 2003.

Carlson, Richard. *The Don't Sweat Guide for Newlyweds: Finding What Matters Most in the First Year.* Hyperion, 2003.

Lee, Jenny. *I Do. I Did. Now What?! Life After the Wedding Dress.* Workman, 2003.

Stark, Marg. *What No One Tells the Bride.* Hyperion, 1998.

PARENTING BOOKS

Hartley-Brewer, Elizabeth. *Raising Confident Boys: 100 Tips for Parents and Teachers.* Fisher Books, 2001.

———. *Raising Confident Girls: 100 Tips for Parents and Teachers.* Fisher Books, 2001.

Stark, Marg. *What No One Tells the Mom: Surviving the Early Years of Parenthood with Your Sanity, Your Sex Life, and Your Sense of Humor Intact*. Perigee, 2005.

Wallerstein, Judith, and Sandra Blakeslee. *What About the Kids? Raising Your Children Before, During and After Divorce*. Hyperion, 2003.

same baggage about stepmothers that our generation and the ones before us did. There's no Cinderella complex for them to get over. No "Snow White" "mirror, mirror" to face. Certainly, some children still read the famous fairy tales, but their personal encounters with stepmothers far outweigh the ones they are exposed to in the antiquated stories about witches and dwarfs. They have enough real-life stepmothers from which to draw their own conclusions.

This business of trying to be something other than "step" seems odd. It's confusing to people who want a quick summary of who's who in your family, and it does nothing to stamp out the stigma of "step." To my friend Ann and the other women out there who reject the term, I say, get over it and learn to embrace the role and title with pride. After all, with over half of all families in the United States claiming step status, there is nothing more *all-American* than a modern stepfamily.

I love my stepchildren, and I love being a stepmother. Every day I feel blessed that the big stepmother in the sky saw something in me that she thought would translate well for the job. It's been a wild ride, but it has been a fun one, too—one that I wouldn't trade for all the shoes, vacations, and spa treatments in the world.

I have a silly thought that one day the people in charge in Hollywood and on Madison Avenue will catch on to the stepmother thing and realize that we're no longer in the minority. We're not wart-nosed and evil. In fact, we're pretty cool. They'll put us in commercials and movies and all of a sudden being a stepmother will be the hottest trend. Single women all over the world will be lining up for the job to help raise someone's first family, and being a stepmother will become as fashionable as tattoos and body piercing. OK, maybe that's a stretch, but it's only a matter of time before we stepmothers start to see ourselves as someone other than the wicked stepmother in a fairy tale. Until then, keep your head up and wear the title proudly, because it's not every day a woman gets the chance to become someone's stepmother.

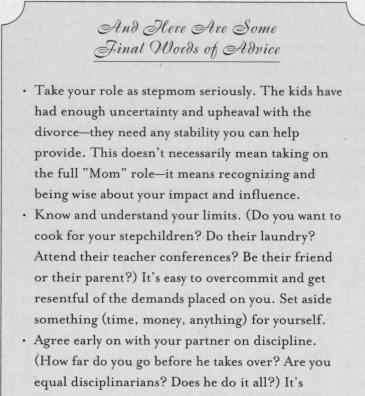

And Here Are Some Final Words of Advice

- Take your role as stepmom seriously. The kids have had enough uncertainty and upheaval with the divorce—they need any stability you can help provide. This doesn't necessarily mean taking on the full "Mom" role—it means recognizing and being wise about your impact and influence.
- Know and understand your limits. (Do you want to cook for your stepchildren? Do their laundry? Attend their teacher conferences? Be their friend or their parent?) It's easy to overcommit and get resentful of the demands placed on you. Set aside something (time, money, anything) for yourself.
- Agree early on with your partner on discipline. (How far do you go before he takes over? Are you equal disciplinarians? Does he do it all?) It's important that you back each other up—but that's just good parenting.

- Make sure the "Respect your stepmom" message comes in loud and clear from their dad. Some dads feel guilty about the situation their kids are in and let their kids behave in a way that is inappropriate. It doesn't set a good example for the kids, and it could make your life miserable. You deserve respect!
- When it comes to developing a relationship with your stepchildren, allow them to take the lead. Try not to be pushy or forceful; instead let your relationship develop naturally. Once you earn your stepchildren's trust, let them know that you will always be there for them.
- Never bad-mouth their mom—directly or subtly.
- Make your bedroom off-limits to the kids.
- Never lose your sassy stepmother sense of humor!

Stark, Marg. *What No One Tells the Mom: Surviving the Early Years of Parenthood with Your Sanity, Your Sex Life, and Your Sense of Humor Intact*. Perigee, 2005.

Wallerstein, Judith, and Sandra Blakeslee. *What About the Kids? Raising Your Children Before, During and After Divorce*. Hyperion, 2003.

Estess, Patricia Schiff. *Money Advice for Your Successful Remarriage: Handling Delicate Financial Issues Intelligently and Lovingly.* ASJA Press, 2001.

Goodman, Karon Phillips. *The Stepmom's Guide to Simplifying Your Life.* Equilibrium Press, 2002.

Keenan, Barbara Mullen. *When You Marry a Man with Children: How to Put Your Marriage First and Stay in Love.* Pocket, 1992.

Millian, Lenore Fogelson, and Stephen Jerry Millian. *The Second Wives Club: Secrets for Becoming Lovers for Life.* Beyond Words, 1999.

Mulford, Philippa Greene. *Keys to Successful Stepmothering.* Barron's, 1996.

Norwood, Perdita Kirkness, and Teri Wingender. *The Enlightened Stepmother, Revolutionizing the Role.* Avon, 1999.

NEWLYWED ADVICE BOOKS

Bliss, Sara. *The Thoroughly Modern Married Girl: Staying Sensational After Saying "I Do."* Broadway Books, 2003.

Bourland, Julia. *Hitched: The Go-Girl Guide to the First Year of Marriage.* Atria Books, 2003.

Carlson, Richard. *The Don't Sweat Guide for Newlyweds: Finding What Matters Most in the First Year.* Hyperion, 2003.

Lee, Jenny. *I Do. I Did. Now What?! Life After the Wedding Dress.* Workman, 2003.

Stark, Marg. *What No One Tells the Bride.* Hyperion, 1998.

PARENTING BOOKS

Hartley-Brewer, Elizabeth. *Raising Confident Boys: 100 Tips for Parents and Teachers.* Fisher Books, 2001.

———. *Raising Confident Girls: 100 Tips for Parents and Teachers.* Fisher Books, 2001.

www.stepfam.org The official Web site of the Stepfamily Association of America, the largest national organization interested in stepfamilies and stepfamily issues.

www.stepfamily.net According to this site, "The Stepfamily Network is a nonprofit organization dedicated to helping stepfamily members achieve harmony and mutual respect in their family lives through education and support."

www.stepmomgroup.com A good general site for stepmothers. Advice and information about topics from knowing your legal rights to keeping the romance with your husband are covered. Nonfee registration required.

www.StepMothers.org A virtual chapter of the Stepfamily Association of America, with a message board and chat room, as well as other resources.

www.yourstepfamily.com *Your Stepfamily* is a magazine for the evolving stepfamily. Real solutions, credible advice, and problem-solving strategies.

Good General Books on Stepparenting and Remarriage

The following is a list of "stepmother-approved books" that have proved to be enlightening and comforting for the single girl turned sassy stepmother and wife.

Bloch-Jones, Merry, and Jo Ann Schiller. *Stepmothers: Keeping It Together with Your Husband and His Kids*. Birch Lane Press, 1992.

www.bonusfamilies.com Dedicated to the support and reassurance of every member of the stepfamily. Contains advice and interesting and helpful articles.

www.co-family.com Producers of a line of greeting cards for cofamilies.

www.comamas.com Teaches ex-wives and stepmothers to get along for the sake of the children. This site offers an active message board, a chat room, advice, and a newsletter. Registration fee required for membership.

www.cyberparent.com/step A general family site with a special section for new stepparents.

www.familyfusion.com A Yahoo site with chat room, boards, bookshop, newsletter, resources, products, and articles.

www.FamiliesInStep.org The Step Family Forum is provided for all members of stepfamilies who would like a useful tool to effectively help them navigate the unique dynamics experienced by stepfamilies by enabling them to share their experience with what works and doesn't in their stepfamily.

www.ivillage.com A women's-lifestyle site that includes information and advice on stepmothering.

www.secondwivescafe.com A fun site with interesting essays from other stepmoms. Good advice and resources for the fledgling stepmother.

www.secondwivesclub.com A well-developed site that has weekly advice from a variety of sources as well as tips, products, book reviews, etc.

www.stepcarefully.com A Christian site provided by MSN with a newsletter and books for review and sale.

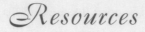

Resources

Associations and Their Web Sites

There are more than a dozen Web sites devoted specifically to stepfamilies and stepmothers where you can read articles, buy books, and meet other stepmothers. In addition, sites such as ivillage.com and LHJ.com (*Ladies' Home Journal*'s Web site) have sections dedicated to stepparenting.

STEPMOTHER AND STEPFAMILY WEB SITES AND ORGANIZATIONS

www.aamft.org/index nm.asp American Association for Marriage and Family Therapy. A general resource for finding a family therapist near you, includes links and book recommendations for families and stepfamilies.

www.babyzone.com A general "mother" Web site with a special section for stepmothers.

www.blendedfamily.com This site contains a parenting Q and A, guest book, message board, surveys, and book list.